# APPURTENANT TO THE
# BIBLIOPHILIC DOMINION OF

---

**BOOKS THAT MAKE YOU SMILE**

"This book is loosely based on a true
story and all truths are false."

-Albert B. Squid

# SQUARE ROOT OF SQUID
# PUBLISHING

BOOK CONCEPT BY: ALBERT B. SQUID
ILLUSTRATIONS/WRITING BY: ALBERT B. SQUID
COVER DESIGN BY: HANNES KLEIN/jkdtp

# PREFACE

Who wants to study boring vocabulary words?
Nobody!!! That's who. But what if learning new words
was fun and easy? That's exactly what this book,
Bigger & Fancier Words That Might Make You Smarter..er
(+ really long subtitle here), is for. This book is
designed for you to learn only one word in one day.
So instead of trying to remember a list of words
at the same time, with only one big & fancy word a
day you can really let that word sink into your
brain, remember the definition throughout the day,
you can use that word in real conversations you
have that day, and see and hear that word used
in books, movies, or when eavesdropping on people.
This book contains one word a day for 366 days of
the year (that's right, leap year is included too),
that you can learn every day or skip days. Each
page is dated, so depending on which date you turn
to in the book, that's the word of that day. Each
page comes with the word of the day, its type, its
meaning, a funny example sentence, and synonyms
and antonyms. Throw this book on the back of the
toilet, in your car, on the coffee table, or next to
your bed, in your underwear drawer, in your
private jet, in the shed, or wherever you do daily
things. Build your vocabulary, study for the SATs,
or gain skills for word games and crossword
puzzles, but do it slow and easy and possibly with a
chuckle here or there.

                                        -Albert B. Squid

(noun)

# ELEUTHEROMANIA

An intense desire for

freedom. MEANING

EXAMPLE

Janet's eleutheromania was so extreme that she decided to live in a treehouse to escape the tyrannical rule of her toaster oven.

SIMILAR

freedom obsession, liberty craze

OPPOSITE

compliance, submission

(noun)

# LACHANOPHOBIA

## The fear of vegetables.

MEANING

EXAMPLE

His lachanophobia was so severe that he would break out into a cold sweat at the sight of a carrot.

SIMILAR

vegetable phobia, veggie fear

OPPOSITE

vegetable love, veggie adoration

(adjective)

# BYSSACEOUS

MEANING

## Looking like thin thread.

EXAMPLE

The balding man had only a few byssaceous hairs left on his head but made good use of them by gelling them into the shape of a hat.

SIMILAR

fibrous, threadlike

OPPOSITE

coarse, thick, rough

(Adverb)

# ACROSTICALLY

Referring to a poem or puzzle in which certain letters in each line form a word or phrase when read vertically. MEANING

EXAMPLE

He wrote his resignation letter acrostically, spelling out 'I QUIT' with the first letter of each line.

SIMILAR

poetically rhythmically

OPPOSITE

incoherently disorganizedly

# JAN 5

(Adjective)

# ATRAMENTOUS

Black or ink-like in color.

My attempt at cooking turned the soup into an atramentous sludge resembling a failed science experiment.

ebony, sable

alabaster, ivory

(noun)

# AZACYANINE

MEANING

Synthetic dyes used in various applications.

EXAMPLE

I spilled the azacyanine dye on my shirt, and now it looks like a psychedelic unicorn puked on me.

SIMILAR

dye, pigment

OPPOSITE

colorless, transparent

(adverb)

# HEBDOMADALLY

MEANING

## Happening every seven days; weekly.

EXAMPLE

I promised to do my laundry hebdomadally, but my pile of dirty clothes is starting to resemble a modern art installation.

SIMILAR

weekly, every seven days

OPPOSITE

randomly, infrequently

(noun)

# GLOSSOPHOBIA

The fear or anxiety of public speaking or speaking in front of an audience.

MEANING

EXAMPLE

John's glossophobia was so severe that even the thought of ordering pizza over the phone made him pee his pants.

SIMILAR

stage fright, public speaking anxiety

OPPOSITE

eloquence, confidence

(noun)

# AXODENDRITE

A neuron's branch that receives signals from other neurons.

MEANING

EXAMPLE

When my brain's axodendrites are overloaded, I start daydreaming about my dog's secret life as a cat.

SIMILAR

neuron, nerve cell

OPPOSITE

non-neuronal, non-nervous

(verb)

# ENCHAFE

---

**MEANING** To cause irritation, annoyance, or frustration.

---

EXAMPLE

My little sister has mastered the art of enchafing me with her constant requests for a dress-up tea party. I like dressing up but I hate invisible tea.

SIMILAR

irritate, annoy

OPPOSITE

please, delight

(noun)

# SECTARIANISM

## Excessive attachment to a particular group.

The rivalry between fans of the two bowling alleys had escalated to the point of sectarianism, with each side fiercely defending their favorite bowling ball size.

partisanship, factionalism

inclusivity, unity

(noun)

# ENJAMBEMENT

The continuation of a sentence without a pause beyond the end of a line in poetry.

My attempt at writing poetry resulted in a chaotic enjambement that made my English teacher jump out the window. Thank goodness we are on the ground floor!

poetry, verse

prose, rhyme

# JAN 13

(adjective)

# DUBITATIVE

Doubtful or hesitating in belief or opinion.

I had a dubitative moment when I saw a pigeon wearing a tuxedo and realized that birds are slaves to fashion just as we are.

skeptical, doubtful

convinced, certain

(adjective)

# CATECHUMENAL

Relating to the period of preparation for baptism or confirmation in Christian religions. MEANING

MEANING

EXAMPLE

I had a catechumenal level of confusion when I went to church for the first time and mistook holy water for a refreshing drink and the collection plate money as a gift to me.

SIMILAR

religious, devotional

OPPOSITE

secular, non-religious

# JAN 15

(adjective)

# DRAMATURGICAL

Relating to the art and technique of dramatic composition.

My family's dinner conversations often take on a dramaturgical tone, complete with dramatic pauses and monologues, ending with an encore of song and dance.

theatrical, dramatic

natural, unscripted

(noun)

# enramada

A shelter or structure made of branches.

I attempted to build an enramada in my backyard, but it ended up looking more like a bird's nest on stilts.

arbor, pergola

clearing, open space

(adjective)

# ORYZIVOROUS

Referring to an animal that eats rice.

The mischievous mouse had developed a rather peculiar taste, becoming oryzivorous and raiding the pantry for all the rice cakes.

rice-eating, grain-eating

non-rice-eating, non-grain-eating

(noun (plural))

# KLEPTOCRACIES

Systems of government or societies in which those in power steal resources. MEANING

EXAMPLE

In the land of Kleptocracies, the national anthem is a catchy tune titled 'Steal My Heart and Everything Else!'.

SIMILAR

corrupt regimes, pilfering governments

OPPOSITE

just governments, transparent administrations

**JAN 19**

(adjective)

# DIVERTICULATED

Having small pouch-like
protrusions or branches.

My inflatable couch turned out to be
more diverticulated than I expected,
resembling a blow-up octopus with
seating options.

branched, forked

straight, linear

(adjective)

# xenocentric

Describing someone or something that is focused on foreign things.

Bill's obsession with collecting exotic souvenirs made him the most xenocentric person in the neighborhood, with a living room resembling a mini-museum of oddities.

exocentric, foreign-oriented

ethnocentric, local-focused

(noun)

# emulousness

MEANING

A strong desire to equal or surpass others in achievement.

EXAMPLE

My emulousness in a pancake-eating contest led to a syrupy mess and a disapproving stare from the pancake chef.

SIMILAR

ambition, competitiveness

OPPOSITE

contentment, indifference

(adjective)

# RAPACIOUS

MEANING

Greedy, voracious, or excessively grasping.

EXAMPLE

My pet spider has a rapacious appetite for pocket lint and will do anything to stockpile it, including stealing some from my pocket.

SIMILAR

greedy, voracious

OPPOSITE

generous, selfless

# JAN 23

(adjective)

# FLAGELLIFEROUS

MEANING

Being whip-like in structure.

EXAMPLE

My cat's tail, equipped with a flagelliferous charm, has become his secret weapon for demanding treats and asserting feline dominance.

SIMILAR

appendage-like, lash-bearing

OPPOSITE

smooth, unadorned

# NYCTOPHOBIA (noun)

The extreme or irrational fear of darkness or the night.

MEANING

EXAMPLE

John's nyctophobia was so intense that he insisted on sleeping with a nightlight shaped like a disco ball.

SIMILAR

achluophobia, noctiphobia

OPPOSITE

nyctophilia (love of darkness), fearlessness

# JAN 25

(adjective)

# DITRIGONAL

Having two sets of three angles each.

My attempt at constructing a ditrigonal sandwich tower failed spectacularly, resulting in a leaning, lopsided mess of ingredients.

triangular, trilateral

circular, spherical

(adjective)

# FLORIFeROUS

Describing something that is bearing many flowers.

EXAMPLE

The floriferous plant took its role as the neighborhood's flower ambassador a bit too seriously, showering unsuspecting pedestrians with a colorful bouquet.

SIMILAR

blooming, blossoming

OPPOSITE

barren, bare

(adjective)

# empleomania

## MEANING

An intense or excessive desire for work.

## EXAMPLE

My empleomania reached such heights that I started dreaming about spreadsheets and having exciting adventures in the world of PowerPoint presentations.

## SIMILAR

workaholism, obsession with work

## OPPOSITE

laziness, indolence

# AZOTOBACTER (noun)

A type of soil-dwelling bacteria.

MEANING

EXAMPLE

The azotobacter bacteria in my garden have formed a miniature nitrogen-fixing army, equipped with tiny shovels and army helmets.

SIMILAR

nitrogen-fixing bacteria, soil bacteria

OPPOSITE

non-bacterial, non-microbial

# JAN 29

(adjective)

# motoneuronal

Pertaining to motor neurons, that transfer signals from the brain to muscles.

I tried to impress my friends by flexing my motoneuronal skills, but ended up inadvertently twitching like a malfunctioning robot.

motor neuron-related, nerve cell-associated

non-neuronal, non-motor

# enclitic (adjective)

Describing a word that is grammatically dependent on a preceding word.

The enclitic word "yo" attached itself to every sentence I spoke, turning me into a linguistic rapper without my consent.

attached, affixed

independent, detached

# JAN 31

(adjective)

# BASURAL

Relating to or resembling a trash heap.

The basural smell was so overpowering that even the flies were considering wearing gas masks.

trashy, garbage filled

clean, tidy

(noun)

# FRUSTOCONICAL

Shaped like a cone that has been cut at the top.

The frustrated ice cream cone decided to undergo a radical transformation and become frustoconical, hoping to stand out among its cylindrical companions.

conical, truncated

cylindrical, spherical

(noun)

# VALETUDINARIAN

## MEANING

A person who is excessively concerned about their health.

## EXAMPLE

The valetudinarian, armed with hand sanitizer and a face mask, believed that the mere sight of a common cold could knock them off their feet.

## SIMILAR

hypochondriac, neurotic

## OPPOSITE

healthy individual, robust person

(verb) # CAIQUEJEE

To speak or argue loudly and forcefully. MEANING

EXAMPLE

During the heated debate, the politicians caiquejeed, their voices clashing like cymbals in an orchestra of chaos.

SIMILAR

shout, bellow

OPPOSITE

whisper, mutter

(adjective)

# CYTOLOGICAL

MEANING

Relating to the branch of biology that studies cells.

## EXAMPLE

The scientist, with a microscope and a passion for cytological exploration, embarked on a cellular adventure that would make any mitochondria jealous.

## SIMILAR

cellular, histological

## OPPOSITE

macroscopic, organismal

(adjective)

# IMPERCIPIENT

Lacking perception or insight.
Unaware.

Despite the giant 'Wet Floor' sign, the impercipient individual confidently slid across the freshly mopped floor, much to the amusement of onlookers.

oblivious, inattentive

perceptive, observant

(adjective)

# SAPONACEOUS

## MEANING

Having the qualities of soap;

soapy.

## EXAMPLE

As the clumsy chef dropped an entire bottle of olive oil into the dish, the sauce took on a saponaceous texture, leading to a slippery dinner disaster.

## SIMILAR

sudsy, lathery

## OPPOSITE

unscented, dry

(adjective)

# ADDUCEABLE

Capable of being offered as evidence or proof. *MEANING*

*EXAMPLE*

The lawyer, armed with a stack of adduceable evidence, confidently approached the courtroom, ready to argue the case of the missing cookie jar.

*SIMILAR*

citable, provable

*OPPOSITE*

inadmissible, unproven

(adjective)
# PUNCTILIOUS

Following all the rules exactly.

## EXAMPLE

Sam was so punctilious about playing musical chairs that he measured the spaces in between chairs and made his own mix tape.

## SIMILAR

careful, meticulous, precise

## OPPOSITE

careless, sloppy, negligent

(noun)

# BARASINGHA

A large deer found in the Indian subcontinent.

The barasingha, with its extravagant antlers resembling a chandelier gone wild, was the envy of all the other deer at the forest fashion show.

swamp deer, eld's deer

antlerless deer, doe

# FEB 10

(adjective)

# LINACEOUS

MEANING

Resembling or relating to flax or linen.

EXAMPLE

When the fashion show started, the models strutted down the runway in linaceous outfits, turning heads and causing a few flax-tuations of excitement among the audience.

SIMILAR

flaxen lignified

OPPOSITE

synthetic non-textile

# VALVULATE

(adjective)

Having valves.

The **valvulate** toaster created perfectly toasted bread, as if it had tiny valves regulating the toasting process.

valve-like, valve-shaped

non-valvular, valveless

# FEB 12

(adjective)

# GERONTOMORPHIC

Resembling an elderly person.

The gerontomorphic boy leisurely lounged in the sun, occasionally complaining about modern technology.

senescent, aged

youthful, juvenile

(adjective)

# NIDULARIACEOUS

Resembling a bird's nest.

The chef carefully arranged the ingredients in a nidulariaceous fashion on the plate, creating a nest-like presentation, complete with pheasant eggs and a cream sauce.

nest-like, nesting

non-nidulariaceous, nest-less

# FEB 14

(noun)

# VALENTINIANISM

A philosophical school of thought associated with Valentinus.

Casey was so passionate about Valentinianism that he insisted on giving out heart-shaped chocolates and gnostic wisdom on Valentine's Day, much to the confusion of his friends.

gnosticism, valentinus' teachings

non-valentinianism, orthodox christianity

(noun)

# LIBEROSIS

The desire to stop caring.

MEANING

EXAMPLE

Struck by liberosis, I wish I had lived in the past until I remembered there were no video games.

SIMILAR

meloncholy, depressed

OPPOSITE

satisfaction, detachment

# SOMATIZATION (noun)

MEANING

Conversion of an emotional problem into physical symptoms.

EXAMPLE

Alice's extreme fear of cucumbers resulted in somatization, causing her to develop a spontaneous cat-like inspired tap dance routine whenever she saw one.

SIMILAR

conversion disorder, psychosomatic

OPPOSITE

non-somatization, mental awareness

(adjective)

# INTERCOLUMNIATION

The spacing between columns.

EXAMPLE

The architect was so obsessed with intercolumniation that she designed a building with columns so close together that it didn't allow for overweight people to pass through.

SIMILAR

column spacing, inter-column distance

OPPOSITE

column clustering, no intercolumniation

(adverb)

# sententiously

## MEANING

Using only a small number of words in a powerful way.

## EXAMPLE

Dave sententiously proclaimed, "One who goes to bed with an itchy butt wakes up with a stinky finger."

## SIMILAR

didactically, preachily

## OPPOSITE

modestly, casually, humbly

(noun) # ASCOLICHEN

A type of lichen.

The ascolichen and moss formed a partnership so strong that they were considering starting a botanical detective agency to solve plant-related crimes.

mossy lichen, lichen-moss

non-ascolichen, lichen-free

# FEB 20

(noun)

# CASTIGATORY

MEANING

Inclined to criticize or reprimand severely.

EXAMPLE

The castigatory librarian shushed patrons with such intensity that books trembled on the shelves and characters in novels apologized for making noise.

SIMILAR

Scolding, reprimanding

OPPOSITE

praiseful, encouraging

# JOCUNDITY (noun)

MEANING

The state of being cheerful.

EXAMPLE

Jumping up and down like a kangaroo on a trampoline, his jocundity was so contagious that even the grumpy grandfather cracked a smile.

SIMILAR

mirthfulness, joviality

OPPOSITE

melancholy, gloominess

(adjective)

# UNOSTENTATIOUS

Not showy or flamboyant; modest.

He arrived at the party in an unostentatious looking suit, so plain and simple that a fashion detective mistook him for a secret agent in disguise.

discreet, unpretentious

ostentatious, flashy

(noun) # Nescience

Lack of knowledge;

ignorance. *MEANING*

*EXAMPLE*

His nescience was legendary; he firmly believed that the Earth was flat because he believes everything famous athletes say.

*SIMILAR*

unawareness, obliviousness

*OPPOSITE*

knowledge, awareness

# FEB 24

# BARONETICAL

Relating to low-ranking hereditary title in the UK.

With his baronetical charm and a monocle that never stayed in place, he tried to knight his pet goldfish as 'Sir Sugar Bubbles" but was thwarted by a rebellious water squirt.

aristocratic, noble

commoner, plebeian

(adjective)

# OLIGOSPERMATIC

Relating to a low sperm count.

As the fertility doctor explained the oligospermatic condition, the sperm specimens in the lab performed synchronized swimming routines to prove that they may be few, but they're full of determination.

sperm-deficient, subfertile

sperm-rich, fertile

# FEB 26

(adjective)

# PINACEOUS

Relating to pine trees or their sap.

MEANING

EXAMPLE

During the camping trip, they discovered that the pinaceous forest had a secret club for pinecones, and they were all eagerly awaiting the annual Pinecone Pageant.

SIMILAR

resinous, piney

OPPOSITE

non-resinous, non-aromatic

(adjective) # VINOUS

Having the qualities of wine. *MEANING*

*EXAMPLE*

At the wine-tasting event, the sommelier proudly proclaimed, 'This chardonnay is so vinous, it can make a grape blush and turn into a raisin within seconds!'

*SIMILAR*

oenophilic, wine-like

*OPPOSITE*

non-alcoholic, non-intoxicating

(noun)

# TAPHONOMIST

MEANING

A scientist who studies the processes of fossilization.

EXAMPLE

The eccentric taphonomist had a habit of whispering secrets to fossils, hoping they would reveal ancient mysteries during midnight picnics with dinosaurs.

SIMILAR

paleontologist, archaeologist

OPPOSITE

uneducated loafer

(adjective)

# EMBOLISMIC

Pertaining to an inserted day in a calendar.

My cat seems to have mastered the embolismic art of inserting extra nap days into my schedule.

intercalary, leap-year

regular, non-leap year

(noun)

# FUMITORY

A group of flowering plants with climbing stems.

MEANING

EXAMPLE

Why did the weed go to therapy? Because it had a fumitory complex!

SIMILAR

climbing corydalis, earth smoke

OPPOSITE

grounded plants, stationary plants

(adjective)

# TERATOGENIC

Factors that can cause birth defects.

Did you hear about the potion that turns people into chickens? It was teratogenic-coop!

developmental abnormalities, reproductive toxicity

non-mutagenic, beneficial

(verb)

# SANGUIFY

To transform or convert into blood.

The magician waved his wand and sanguified a tomato, turning it into a bloody mary.

blood change, blood transformation

unchanged, deplete blood

(noun)

# DEFENESTRATION

The act of throwing someone or something out

MEANING of a window.

EXAMPLE

The defenestration of my alarm clock was a satisfying way to start the day.

SIMILAR

ejection, dismissal

OPPOSITE

entry, welcome

(noun)

# EPIPHONEMA

A witty remark that ends a conversation.

MEANING

EXAMPLE

He concluded the debate with an epiphonema which was that shrimp are just ocean cockroaches.

SIMILAR

epigram, quip

OPPOSITE

rambling, anticlimax

(noun)

# LOGOMACHY

An argument about words or their meanings. MEANING

EXAMPLE

The logomachy between the linguist and the pun master escalated into a fierce thumb war.

SIMILAR

verbal sparring, lexical debate

OPPOSITE

agreement, harmony

(noun)

# TINTINNABULATION

The ringing or sound of bells.

The tintinnabulation of the alarm clock turned the morning wake-up call into a chaotic symphony of jolts and curses.

bell chime, bell clangor

silence, stillness

(noun)
# PLUVIOPHILE

## A person who loves

MEANING rain.

EXAMPLE

The pluviophile danced joyfully in the pouring rain, much to the confusion of the neighborhood cats seeking shelter.

SIMILAR

rain lover, rain enthusiast

OPPOSITE

heliophile (sun lover), xerophobe (rain hater)

# EUNOIA (noun)

## Goodwill towards others.

Bob's eunoia was so strong that he couldn't resist bringing cookies to his neighbor's pet rock on its birthday.

benevolence, amicability

animosity, hostility

(noun)

# ULTRACREPIDARIAN

A person who advises on matters beyond their knowledge.

*MEANING*

EXAMPLE

The ultracrepidarian confidently lectured the physicists on the art of time travel using only a broken pocket watch and a can of beans.

SIMILAR

pompous pontificator, bluffer

OPPOSITE

specialist, humble learner

(adjective)

# CALLIPYGIAN

MEANING

Having beautifully shaped buttocks.

EXAMPLE

Her callipygian figure made it hard to pass through some doorways.

SIMILAR

shapely, curvaceous

OPPOSITE

flat, shapeless

(adjective)

# SEMPITERNAL

Lasting forever;

MEANING eternal.

EXAMPLE

My dog's love for bacon is sempiternal; he'll sing opera for a strip!

SIMILAR

perpetual, timeless

OPPOSITE

temporary, finite

(adjective)

# SUSURROUS

Producing whispering or rustling sounds.

MEANING

EXAMPLE

The suspect's attempt to be stealthy was thwarted by the susurrous sound of their snack bag.

SIMILAR

whispering, rustling

OPPOSITE

rowdy, loud

(adjective)

# XANTHOMELANOUS

To have a yellow or yellowish-brown coloration.

MEANING

EXAMPLE

The fashion world was taken by storm when the xanthomelanous collection hit the runway, turning models into walking sunshine and butterscotch candies.

SIMILAR

flavomelanous, chromochalchous

OPPOSITE

achromic, melanistic

# PSITHURISM (noun)

MEANING

The sound of wind rustling through trees.

EXAMPLE

The trees engaged in a lively conversation of psithurism, gossiping about the mischievous squirrels and singing praises of them.

SIMILAR

silence, noise

OPPOSITE

whispers, rustling

(adjective)

# AILUROPHILE

A person who loves cats.

As an ailurophile, I have embraced a life full of purr-sonalities, whisker tickles, and endless supplies of lint rollers.

cat lover, felinophile

ailurophobe, cat hater

# MAR 17

(noun)

# BUMBERSHOOT

A humorous term for an umbrella.

Carrying a bumbershoot on a sunny day is like wearing a snorkel in a desert—it's all about being prepared for the unexpected!

umbrella, sunshade

parasol, canopy

(verb)

# QUOMODOCUNQUIZE

To make money by any possible means.

MEANING

EXAMPLE

Jack had such a knack for quomodocunquize that he started a business selling personalized pet rocks with built-in microchips for a hefty price.

SIMILAR

to hustle, excell

OPPOSITE

lazy, loser

# MAR 19

(noun)
# PHILTRUM

The vertical groove between the nose and the upper lip.

After taking a sip of hot soup, George realized his philtrum was the perfect soup-draining channel, making him the envy of all messy eaters.

median groove, facial groove

cleft lip, smooth lip

# ZARF (noun)

MEANING

A holder or sleeve used to protect hands from hot beverages.

EXAMPLE

Sandra realized her collection of zarfs had gotten out of hand when she couldn't find her actual coffee mug beneath the tower of colorful, knitted hand protectors.

SIMILAR

cozy, sleeve

OPPOSITE

bare hands, insulated mug

**MAR 21**

(adverb)

# RETROMINGENTLY

Referring to the act of urinating backward.

While most cats prefer to urinate in a litter box, Mr. Whiskers took a retromingently rebellious approach, aiming for the toilet seat with surprising accuracy.

backwardly, reversely

forwardly, normally

(adjective)

# BUTYRACEOUS

MEANING

Having the qualities or characteristics of butter, such as being smooth, creamy, or having a butter-like texture.

EXAMPLE

The toast was so perfectly golden and crisp, even the pickiest of breakfast enthusiasts couldn't resist slathering it with butyraceous delight.

SIMILAR

butter-like, creamy

OPPOSITE

crumbly, dry

# MAR 23

(noun)

# LETHOLOGICA

The inability to recall a specific word or name.

During the spelling bee, Tammy was struck by a sudden case of lethologica, causing her to blurt out a nonsensical word that left both the judges and audience shocked.

anomia, word-finding difficulty

fluent, articulate

# (noun) VERBOMANIA

An excessive or obsessive MEANING use of words.

EXAMPLE

If you bought this book and are reading this sentence now you may suffer from verbomania when you have your next conversation.

SIMILAR

verbophilia, verbal hyperactivity

OPPOSITE

agraphia, Aphasia

(noun)

# MONACHOPSIS

The feeling that you don't belong.

MEANING

EXAMPLE

I felt monachopsis at the yoga class because nobody was farting except me.

SIMILAR

alienation, displacement

OPPOSITE

belonging, harmony

(adjective)

# EFFULGENT

MEANING

## Shining brilliantly; radiant.

EXAMPLE

Greg's newly polished head reflected the sunlight with such effulgence that nearby birds mistook him for a disco ball and started dancing around him.

SIMILAR

radiant, luminous

OPPOSITE

dull, gloomy

(noun)

# CASTRAMETATION

The planning and setting up of a military camp.

With unmatched castrametation skills, the squirrel scouts transformed a patch of park into a perfectly organized acorn fortress, complete with tiny tents and nut-filled rations.

encampment, campcraft

disbandment, demobilization

# ZEPHYRIAN (adjective)

Something or someone related to or resembling a gentle, mild breeze.

Tyler's hair was so expertly styled that it appeared perpetually zephyrian, even amid a hurricane!

breezy, airy

blustery, stormy

(adjective)

# EUPHONIOUS

| |
|---|
| Having a pleasant MEANING sound. |

MEANING

EXAMPLE

The cat's meow was so euphonious that it attracted a crowd of music-loving mice.

SIMILAR

melodious, harmonious

OPPOSITE

dissonant, discordant

(adjective)

# LAMBENT

## Softly glowing or flickering.

The lambent glow of the refrigerator lured the sleepwalking panda into mistaking it for a portal to the bamboo dimension.

radiant, glowing

dim, dull

**MAR 31**

(verb)

# ELUCUBRATE

To develop an idea in detail.

After hours of elucubrating over the best toppings for his pizza, he finally came up with the genius combination of chocolate and pickles.

expound, explicate

simplify, condense

# ZETETIC (adjective)

Relating to a search for knowledge through investigation.

MEANING

EXAMPLE

The zetetic glutton embarked on a quest to uncover the secret behind disappearing cupcakes.

SIMILAR

investigative, inquisitive

OPPOSITE

accepting, complacent

# PALIMPSEST (noun)

A manuscript that has been partially erased.

MEANING

EXAMPLE

The shopping list turned into a palimpsest as mom's attempts at crossing out items became a chaotic scribble of indecipherable doodles.

SIMILAR

manuscript, document

OPPOSITE

original, unaltered

(adjective)

# QUAQUAVERSAL

MEANING

Extending or dipping in
all directions.

EXAMPLE

Tanner's quaquaversal hairstyle
made him the target of constant
bird nesting attempts.

SIMILAR

omnidirectional, multidirectional

OPPOSITE

unidirectional, one-sided

(adjective)

# CALLITHUMPIAN

MEANING

## Being noisy to the extent of causing aggravation.

EXAMPLE

The callithumpian parade of kazoo-playing cats and accordion-wielding chickens left the entire town in a state of bewildered amusement.

SIMILAR

boisterous, raucous

OPPOSITE

serene, peaceful

(adjective)

# CLINQUANT

Gaudy or glittery in appearance, especially with clothing or ornaments.

MEANING

EXAMPLE

The Maltese puppy strutted down the runway wearing a clinquant tutu, demanding attention and treats.

SIMILAR

sparkling, shiny

OPPOSITE

plain, dull

# SERIATIM (adverb)

## In a series, sequentially.

I carefully organized my sock drawer, separating them seriatim by color, thickness, and a questionable criterion called 'socks I use to make puppets with'.

sequentially, successively

randomly, haphazardly

(adverb)

# WIDDERSHINS

MEANING

In a direction opposite to the sun's course; counterclockwise.

EXAMPLE

Confused by the dance instructions, he spun widdershins and ended up crashing into the punch bowl spilling the liquid it contained on Marge's new white sun dress.

SIMILAR

anticlockwise, counterclockwise

OPPOSITE

clockwise, deasil

(adjective)

# VAGARIOUS

Whimsical in behavior or actions.

His vagarious nature led him to spontaneously adopt a flock of pelicans as pets.

capricious, unpredictable

consistent, predictable

(noun)

# CYNOSURE

A person or thing that is the center of attention.

MEANING

EXAMPLE

The dancing hot dog vendor became the cynosure of the park, drawing crowds of delighted sausage enthusiasts.

SIMILAR

focus, centerpiece

OPPOSITE

inconspicuous, unnoticed

**APR 10**

(adjective)

# QUISQUILIAN

*MEANING*

## Trivial or worthless.

*EXAMPLE*

The quisquilian task of organizing my toenail collection into categories of length and color gave me solace.

*SIMILAR*

insignificant, trifling

*OPPOSITE*

valuable, significant

(verb)

# CACHINNATE

MEANING

## To laugh loudly or uncontrollably.

EXAMPLE

The comedian's jokes were so hilarious that the audience couldn't help but cachinnate, causing them to blow their drinks out of their noses.

SIMILAR

guffaw, chortle

OPPOSITE

sob, weep

(noun)

# MELLILOQUY

## Excessive or melodramatic talk.

Linda's melliloquy about her missing nutcracker reached epic proportions, complete with a dramatic reenactment and a plea for a search party.

verbose, grandiloquence

conciseness, brevity

(noun)

# Sempiternity

Endless duration or eternity.

Waiting for my turn at the DMV felt like a sempiternity, but I finally made it out with my personalized license plate reading "ANUSTART".

perpetuity, infinity

transience, momentariness

(adjective) # EXIMIOUS

MEANING

Distinguished or excellent in skill or talent.

EXAMPLE

Despite her eximious talent for singing in the shower, Jane's performance on stage left the audience covering their ears and questioning the meaning of "talent."

SIMILAR

exceptional, outstanding

OPPOSITE

mediocre, incompetent

(noun) # PHILOMATH

MEANING

## A lover of learning.

EXAMPLE

If you bought this book and/or are reading this sentence right now, you are probably a philomath.

SIMILAR

scholar, intellectual

OPPOSITE

anti-intellectual, ignoramus

(adjective)

# ARACHNOPHAGOUS

Describing things that
eat spiders.

Given that humans eat around forty
spiders while sleeping in a lifetime, we
could be categorized as arachnophagous
beings.

insectivorous, mycophagous

arachnophobic, herbivorous

(noun)

# APPURTENANCE

Something that goes with
something else.

*MEANING*

*EXAMPLE*

The superhero's utility belt contained
several appurtenances, including clean
underwear, a crocheting kit, and nail
polish remover.

*SIMILAR*

add-on, accessory, attachment

*OPPOSITE*

core, main feature, essential

# APR 18

(adjective)

# JENTACULAR

Relating to breakfast or

occurring in the morning.

My jentacular routine involved waking up to the sound of my wife's flatulence, holding my nose, and finally getting relief from the smell of my morning coffee.

morning-related, breakfast-oriented

nocturnal, dinner-related

(noun) # AVIGATION

---

The act of navigating or flying
an aircraft.

*MEANING*

---

*EXAMPLE*

My attempts at avigation during a video
game were so disastrous that even the
virtual birds requested a parachute.

*SIMILAR*

aeronautics, aviation

*OPPOSITE*

terrestrial navigation, land-based
travel

# FRISSON (noun)

A sudden intense feeling, often accompanied by goosebumps.

As the roller coaster plummeted down the steep drop, Jackson experienced a frisson of excitement mixed with regret for choosing to wear a toupee that was now perched precariously on his head.

thrill, shiver

apathy, calmness

(verb)

# GORMANDIZE

## To eat food greedily.

Andy couldn't resist the temptation of the all-you-can-eat buffet and proceeded to gormandize himself into a food coma, much to the amazement of the restaurant staff.

overindulge, gluttonize

moderate, restrict

(noun)

# CACOETHES

A strong desire to do something, often with negative MEANING consequences.

EXAMPLE

Despite having two left feet, Fred couldn't resist the cacoethes to join the dance competition and showcase his "unique" moves.

SIMILAR

compulsion, impulse

OPPOSITE

restraint, aversion

(noun)

# PANDICULATION

The act of stretching and yawning.

Peter's pandiculation during the boring lecture led the professor to realize he sucked at his job.

stretching, yawning

contraction, rigidity

(noun)

# PSITTACISM

MEANING

The repetitive use of another person's words without understanding their meaning.

EXAMPLE

During the game of charades, Irene was so drunk she resorted to psittacism, repeating the same random sounds and gestures over and over.

SIMILAR

parroting, echoing

OPPOSITE

originality, creativity

(adjective)

# MOLLUSCIVOROUS

Relating to someone or something that feeds on mollusks.

MEANING

EXAMPLE

Albert, the molluscivorous cat, proudly declared himself the 'shellfish sheriff' as he patrolled the beach, ensuring no sneaky clams escaped justice.

SIMILAR

mollusk-eating, shellfish-devouring

OPPOSITE

herbivorous (plant-eating), frugivorous (fruit-eating)

# AVOCATION (noun)

A hobby or second job.

Joan's main job was as an accountant, but her avocation was dressing up in furry animal costumes and going to the zoo.

passtime, side hustle

career, profession, livelihood

(noun) **YLEM**

Matter from which the universe is believed to have originated.

MEANING

EXAMPLE

Pierre's attempt to create a gourmet dish using ylem resulted in an explosion that rearranged his kitchen into a chaotic cosmic mess.

SIMILAR

primordial substance, cosmic matter

OPPOSITE

refined material, finished product

(verb)

# BUMFUZZLE

To confuse, perplex, or fluster someone.

Trying to assemble the new furniture without the instructions bumfuzzled Stella, and she ended up with a bookshelf that looked more like an abstract sculpture.

befuddle, confound

clarify, enli

(noun)

# LEXIPHANICISM

The excessive use of pretentious and complex words to show off one's vocabulary. MEANING

EXAMPLE

Jeremy's lexiphanicism was on full display at the party, using words so convoluted he actually came off looking like a supercilious arse.

SIMILAR

verbose language, bombastic speech

OPPOSITE

plain language, simple expression

**APR 30**

(noun)

# euneirophrenia

A pleasant state of mind after a restful dream.

Waking up from a dream where he was a single man, John couldn't help but experience a moment of euneirophrenia before realizing he still had to face the realities of his everyday life.

blissful contentment, dream-induced euphoria

nightmarish distress

(noun)

# SOMNAMBULIST

## A sleepwalker.

MEANING

EXAMPLE

Tom's somnambulist tendencies led him to have a late-night adventure where he rearranged the furniture in his house, thinking he was participating in a secret mission for a top-secret organization.

SIMILAR

sleepwalker, noctambulist

OPPOSITE

wakeful, insomniac

# MAY 2

(noun)

# PARAPROSDOKIAN

A figure of speech where the latter part of a sentence surprises or amuses the reader.

As I eagerly waited for the punchline of the joke, the comedian expertly slipped in a paraprosdokian that caught me so off guard, my laughter ricocheted through the room, startling nearby pigeons into a synchronized, feathered frenzy!

surprise ending, twist of phrase

predictable punchline, straightforward statement

(adjective)

# DOLICHOCEPHALIC

## MEANING

Having a long shaped head.

## EXAMPLE

The dolichocephalic nature of Kevin's cranium led to comments from his peers such as: "Why the long face Kev? Are you sad?".

## SIMILAR

leptocephalic, long-headed

## OPPOSITE

round-headed, brachycephalic

# DYSANIA (noun)

The state of finding it difficult to get out of bed in the morning.

Sarah's dysania was so extreme that her alarm clock developed a complex and started hitting the snooze button for her.

morning lethargy, bedtime struggle

morning energy, early rising

(noun)

# PRESENTIMENT

A feeling something bad is about to happen.

MEANING

EXAMPLE

She was overtaken with a presentiment that the world was ending when her toast popped up with the face of Jesus on it.

SIMILAR

intuition, premonition

OPPOSITE

certainty, assurance

(adjective)

# IRREFRAGABLE

Impossible to dispute or
disprove.

MEANING

EXAMPLE

"If a bear lives in the woods, then
said bear craps in the woods." is an
irrefragable statement.

SIMILAR

undeniable, indisputable

OPPOSITE

disputable, arguable, refutable

(noun)

# DELECTATION

MEANING

Great pleasure.

MEANING

EXAMPLE

After putting itching powder in their uniforms, Sally took great delectation in watching the entire cheerleader squad scratch themselves.

SIMILAR

enjoyment, delight, fun

OPPOSITE

boredom, misery

(noun)

# CLERISY

A group of intellectuals.

The band "Hard Mucus" proclaimed themselves the "Clerisy of Heavy Metal" for their clever lyrics about mucus membranes.

smart people, scholars

idiots, dummies, uneducated

(noun) # FANTASMA

## A ghost.

MEANING

EXAMPLE

The mischievous fantasma stole all the left socks from the laundry, leaving behind a trail of mismatched pairs.

SIMILAR

specter, apparition

OPPOSITE

living being, tangible entity

(verb)

# CATECHIZE

To teach with the use of questions.

The teacher catechized the students by asking, "Do you really think dogs like the taste of homework?".

instruct, quiz,

neglect, ignore, indoctrinate

(noun)

# MELISSOPHOBIA

An intense fear of bees.

MEANING

EXAMPLE

When Jenny spotted a bee, her melissophobia kicked in, and she ran faster than a bee with a caffeine addiction.

SIMILAR

apiphobia (fear of bees), entomophobia (fear of insects)

OPPOSITE

beekeeping enthusiast, bee lover

# SISYPHEAN (noun)

MEANING

Involving endless, futile, or repetitive effort.

EXAMPLE

His attempt to clean the polluted toilet felt sisyphean, as it immediately became clear it would never be white again.

SIMILAR

endless task, futile endeavor

OPPOSITE

accomplished task, successful endeavor

(noun)

# KAFFEEKLATSCH

A group of friends who get together for coffee.

MEANING

EXAMPLE

At our weekly kaffeeklatsch, we discuss everything from the latest gossip to the existential crises of garden gnomes, all while sipping coffee like caffeinated philosophers.

 SIMILAR

coffee morning, coffee talk

OPPOSITE

silent solitude, seclusion

# MAY 14

(adjective)

# UNASINOUS

MEANING

Sharing the same
stupidity within a group.

EXAMPLE

The panel of astronomers'
unasinous remarks that the earth
was flat stunned the priest.

SIMILAR

foolish, unintelligent

OPPOSITE

intelligent, astute

(noun)

# WHIGMALEERIE

A whimsical or fanciful object or notion.

MEANING

EXAMPLE

The art exhibit showcased various whigmaleeries including a urinal filled with yogurt and a giant golden cheeseburger.

SIMILAR

fanciful object, whimsical notion

OPPOSITE

serious object, realistic notion

# MAY 16

(noun)

# xenizaTion

The act of traveling or living as a stranger or foreigner.

MEANING

EXAMPLE

His love for xenization led him to explore new countries while constantly mispronouncing the local cuisine.

SIMILAR

foreign travel, sojourning

OPPOSITE

native residency, homecoming

(adjective)

# ACROAMATIC

Designed for or understood by a select group of knowledgeable people. MEANING

EXAMPLE

The professor's acroamatic lectures left his students bewildered and questioning their career choices.

SIMILAR

esoteric, specialized

OPPOSITE

accessible, general

# MAY 18

(noun)

# BLANDILOQUENCE

Flattering or smooth-talking

MEANING speech.

EXAMPLE

As the politician droned on with his blandiloquence, the audience struggled to keep their eyes open, secretly yearning for a sudden meteorological phenomenon or a spontaneous parade of dancing donkeys to break the monotony.

SIMILAR

flattery, sweet-talking

OPPOSITE

bluntness, straightforwardness

(noun)

# DYSTHYMIA

A persistent mild depression that lasts for an extended period. MEANING

EXAMPLE

His dysthymia made it difficult for him to find joy in even the most cheerful cat videos.

SIMILAR

chronic depression, low mood

OPPOSITE

euphoria, happiness

(adjective)

# FUBSY

Short and stout;
pleasantly plump.

The fubsy man was embarrassed in front of his date when he could not fit in the rollercoaster car seat.

chubby, plump

slender, thin

(adjective)

# GERONTOCRACY

A system or government
ruled by old people.

MEANING

EXAMPLE

The gerontocracy's decision to
reprint all the books in the city
library to large print format irked a
lot of people.

SIMILAR

elder rule, aged governance

OPPOSITE

youth rule, young leadership

# JEREMIAD (noun)

A long, mournful complaint or lamentation.

Her jeremiad about the lack of cumquats served at the cafeteria left her friends questioning the depth of her concerns.

tirade, diatribe

praise, compliment

(noun)

# DRUMMOCK

A small hill or mound of dirt.

MEANING

EXAMPLE

I tripped over a tiny drummock and executed the most awkward tumble of my life filling my mouth with dirt.

SIMILAR

mound, knoll

OPPOSITE

valley, hollow

(adjective)

# MELLIFLUOUS

Sweet or musical- sounding.

Gary, the mellifluous parrot, had such a soothing voice that he was recruited by a sleep clinic to provide after-hours lullabies for thankful patients.

musical, melodious

harsh, cacophonous

(adjective)

# PERISTERONIC

Pertaining to or resembling pigeons.

MEANING

EXAMPLE

She had a peristeronic charm, attracting pigeons wherever she went, much to the amusement of onlookers.

SIMILAR

pigeon-like, dove-like

OPPOSITE

youth rule, young leadership

(adjective)

# RECALCITRANT

Stubbornly resistant to authority or control.

The recalcitrant toddler refused to eat anything except toilet paper much to his parents' frustration.

obstinate, defiant

compliant, obedient

(adjective)

# TeRPSICHOReAN

Relating to dancing.

MEANING

EXAMPLE

At the family reunion, my 99-year-old grandpa proved himself to be the unexpected terpsichorean sensation, wowing everyone with his **wild dance** moves that could make a herd of clumsy elephants look like break dancers in comparison.

SIMILAR

dance-related, choreographic

OPPOSITE

non-dance-related, non-choreographic

(adjective)

# UMBRIFEROUS

Providing shade or

MEANING shadow.

EXAMPLE

Amidst the scorching summer heat, Brian proudly proclaimed himself the 'umbriferous ambassador' as he marched around the beach, donning an oversized umbrella hat that cast a shadow bigger than his ego.

SIMILAR

shady, shadowy

OPPOSITE

sunny, exposed

# VOMITORY (noun)

An entrance or exit, especially a passage in a stadium or theater. MEANING

EXAMPLE

After eating three buckets of popcorn at the movie, Jules suddenly ran toward the vomitory and into the lavatory to puke.

SIMILAR

entrance/exit, passageway

OPPOSITE

enclosed space, dead end

# MAY 30

(noun)

# WINKLEPICKER

A pointed-toe shoe or boot.

He strutted down the street wearing his winklepickers, inadvertently puncturing holes in inflatable decorations along the way.

pointed shoe, needle-toe footwear

rounded shoe, blunt-toe footwear

(noun)

# zenzizenzizenzic

The eighth power of a number.

Mathematicians debated the practicality of zenzizenzizenzic and whether it had any real-world applications beyond causing headaches.

eighth power, mathematical concept

lower power, smaller exponent

# FLORIGEN

(noun)

A substance responsible for flowering in plants.

MEANING

EXAMPLE

The florigen whispered sweet nothings to the daisies, urging them to bloom.

SIMILAR

flower-inducing, bloom-promoting

OPPOSITE

flower-inhibiting, bloom-restraining

(noun)

# OGDOAD

A set of eight things.

Larry was born with an ogdoad of fingers on his right hand, allowing him to play guitar, type a book report, and pick his nose at the same time.

ensemble, octet, eightfold

pair, triad

(adjective)

# exoDIAN

Pertaining to or originating from a foreign land.

MEANING

EXAMPLE

The exodian chef dazzled the locals with exotic dishes like cockroach tacos and earthworm pizza.

SIMILAR

foreign, alien

OPPOSITE

native, local

(noun)

# ZETTABYTE

One sextillion bytes of
digital storage.

I took so many selfies on my
graduation that I filled up my
phone's storage, resulting in a
zettabyte-sized headache for my
poor device!

exabyte, petabyte

kilobyte, megabyte

(adjective)

# CHATOYANT

Having changeable colors.

MEANING

EXAMPLE

Devon's chatoyant shirt was so colorful that it still looked the same even after becoming sick from eating too much candy and pork.

SIMILAR

lustrous, shimmering

OPPOSITE

dull, flat, matte

(adjective)

# PUSILLANIMOUS

Lacking courage and/or
determination.

MEANING

EXAMPLE

The boy's pusillanimous personality
left him without a date for the
prom, forcing him to go single and
dance with the janitor.

SIMILAR

timid, shy, cowardly

OPPOSITE

courageous, confident

(noun)

# entelechy

The realization of potential.

MEANING

EXAMPLE

Sara finally achieved her entelechy in art when she realized she could use fingernails and toenails as the perfect sculpture material rather than wood or metal.

SIMILAR

actualization, fulfillment

OPPOSITE

stagnation, incompleteness

(noun)

# INSOUCIANCE

A carefree attitude.

## EXAMPLE

John's insouciance was on full display while he used the sample toilet on the showroom floor to the disgust of the many onlooking customers.

## SIMILAR

relaxed, nonchalant, chill

## OPPOSITE

anxiety, stress, uptight, tense

(noun)

# CEREBRATION

The act of using the brain to think.

EXAMPLE

After many hours of cerebration and juggling practice, Henry decided to go to college and major in Clown Studies.

SIMILAR

ignorance, carelessness

OPPOSITE

reasoning, contemplation, thinking

(noun)
# SAPIENCE

Having great knowledge.

MEANING

EXAMPLE

My family was well aware of the sapience my grandfather possessed, even if he liked to wear his adult diapers on the outside of his pants.

SIMILAR

wisdom, intelligence, sagacity

OPPOSITE

stupidity, ignorance

(noun)

# IMBROGLIO

## MEANING

A confusing situation.

## EXAMPLE

Christmas Eve became an imbroglio when Uncle Fred showed up in a ball gown and insisted we call him Auntie Freida.

## SIMILAR

quagmire, muddle, entanglement

## OPPOSITE

clarity, solution

(adjective)

# PLETHORIC

Describes a large amount of something.

EXAMPLE

His plethoric collection of superhero masks and rom-com DVDs shows he's courageous and sensitive.

SIMILAR

overabundant, teeming

OPPOSITE

sparse, scant, meager

(noun)

# MALEDICTION

## An evil wish.

After I drank from the milk carton, my mother yelled a string of maledictions so powerful my father's toupee blew off.

curse, hex, spell

blessing, praise

(adjective)

# DILATORY

Slow to act on something.

MEANING

EXAMPLE

His dilatory approach to bathing daily led his coworkers to stuff toilet paper balls up their nostrils at the office.

SIMILAR

procrastinatory, hesitation

OPPOSITE

prompt, efficient

(adjective)

# PRELAPSARIAN

## MEANING

Related to a time before trouble started.

## EXAMPLE

In prelapsarian Rome, life was good, where a citizen didn't have to worry about walking through a vomitorium and stepping in puke.

## SIMILAR

innocent, utopian, peaceful

## OPPOSITE

corrupt, distopian

(adjective)

# eLeemosYNARY

## MEANING

Related to charity.

## EXAMPLE

In the end, Ron's eleemosynary character left him with little money in the bank so he could only afford two maids instead of three.

## SIMILAR

generous, philanthropic

## OPPOSITE

stingy, miserly, selfish

(verb)

# DESQUAMATE

To shed or peel off scales or outer skin layers.

Samantha's attempt at a DIY face mask went hilariously wrong when she unintentionally caused her skin to desquamate, leaving her resembling a flaky pastry more than a beauty guru.

exfoliate, shed

accumulate, retain

(noun)

# EXUNDATION

The act of overflowing or excessive abundance.

MEANING

EXAMPLE

When Liz tried to make pancakes, she accidentally poured too much batter on the griddle, resulting in an exundation of pancake overflow that resembled a fluffy tsunami taking over the kitchen.

SIMILAR

overflow, deluge

OPPOSITE

scarcity, dearth

(verb)

# CORUSCATE

## MEANING

To sparkle with a flashing light.

## EXAMPLE

Uranus coruscated so brightly that it caused the astronaut to fall into a deep trance.

## SIMILAR

gleam, flicker, shine

## OPPOSITE

dull, obscure, dim

# HYPOTHECATE (verb)

To offer something as security for a debt.

MEANING

EXAMPLE

Jim went to extreme measures to prove his loyalty to the pizza delivery guy by hypothecating his collection of rare cheese as collateral for a single slice of pepperoni.

SIMILAR

pledge, collateralize

OPPOSITE

repay, unencumber

(adjective)

# ANALEPTIC

Boosting brain power.

## EXAMPLE

She **was so tired** from shoveling cow poop all **day**, but a few analeptic cocktails soon changed that.

## SIMILAR

revitalizing, restorative

## OPPOSITE

fatiguing, exhausting

(verb)

# eXPOSTULATe

**MEANING**

To argue with someone.

**EXAMPLE**

The wife expostulated about why her husband keeps leaving the toilet seat up, and the husband expostulated why she nags him so much.

**SIMILAR**

protest, disagree, object

**OPPOSITE**

agree, approve, support

(adjective)

# GUILEFUL

MEANING

## Clever and cunning.

EXAMPLE

The guileful vagabond was able to sneak by the storekeepers watch to grab a few handfuls of jellybeans.

SIMILAR

deceitful, sneaky

OPPOSITE

clumsy, awkward

(adjective)

# ILLIMITABLE

Having no limit. Endless.

MEANING

EXAMPLE

Zoe's illimitable allowance from her father allowed her to buy diamond-studded tail warmers for every day of the year for her dog Bitty Boo.

SIMILAR

infinite, boundless, unrestricted

OPPOSITE

limited, finite, restricted

# oenophile (noun)

Someone who loves wine.

MEANING

EXAMPLE

Joe considered himself a bona fide trailer park oenophile thanks to his collection of vintage box wines.

SIMILAR

sommelier, wine enthusiast

OPPOSITE

teetotaler, wine hater

(noun)
# encomium

A speech or writing that praises someone/something highly. MEANING

EXAMPLE

Tom's encomium to his father was awesome, praising him for teaching him the fine art of cockroach farming, truly a legacy to be proud of.

SIMILAR

tribute, eulogy

OPPOSITE

condemnation, criticism

(noun)

# EPITRACHELION

MEANING

A piece of clothing worn by Christian clergy around the neck.

EXAMPLE

Father Elton accidentally mistook his epitrachelion for a superhero cape during the Easter service, making the congregation question whether he was delivering a sermon or about to save the day.

SIMILAR

stole, omophorion

OPPOSITE

layperson, secular attire

(noun)

# monition

MEANING

A warning and/or advice.

EXAMPLE

The plumber gave a monition to his apprentice to show more butt crack or he wouldn't receive his plumbing badge.

SIMILAR

caution, reminder, threat

OPPOSITE

encouragement, approval

(verb)

# ABSQUATULATE

## MEANING

To leave quickly.

## EXAMPLE

The dog absquatulated from the trash-filled kitchen when he heard his owner's car pull in the driveway.

## SIMILAR

flee, bolt, escape, left

## OPPOSITE

linger, stay, remain

(adjective)
# exergonic

Referring to releasing energy.

After eating the pork and beans, there was a huge exergonic event in his pants.

spontaneous, energetic

inactive, energy input

# unisonant (adjective)

In harmony or agreement with.

MEANING

EXAMPLE

The unisonant cheer coming from the bachelorette party was deafening when the male stripper removed his fake police hat, revealing his bald head.

SIMILAR

in sync with, concurring

OPPOSITE

disagreement, disconnected

(adjective)

# SCEPTRED

Having power and/or authority. MEANING

## EXAMPLE

The sceptred school bully held the record for most wedgies in a single school day with 25.

## SIMILAR

king-like, regal, sovereign

## OPPOSITE

powerless, weak, common

## JUL 3

(noun)
# CATHOLICON

### MEANING

A universal remedy.

### EXAMPLE

I read on the internet that rubbing cat urine on your chest before bed was a catholicon for all ailments, but it was a lie, the only thing it helped me with was a divorce.

### SIMILAR

cure-all, panacea, elixir

### OPPOSITE

poison, affliction

(verb)

# GASCONADE

MEANING

To boast or brag.

EXAMPLE

Trent is constantly gasconading about how he is the best at cooking but I think his sushi smoothies and liver pancakes suck.

SIMILAR

bluster, bloviate, vaunt

OPPOSITE

be modest, be humble

(verb)

# ADUMBRATE

## MEANING

To outline briefly.

## EXAMPLE

The bank robber adumbrated the bank job to his partner, leaving out many details like the escape plan and now they are doing hard time.

## SIMILAR

to sketch, evoke

## OPPOSITE

expound, elaborate, detailed speech

(noun)

# BORBORYGMUS

**MEANING**

The gurgling sound of the stomach.

**EXAMPLE**

Before church, Albert ate beans. During the sermon, his borborygmus was so loud it sounded like an exorcism in his stomach.

**SIMILAR** grumble, rumble

**OPPOSITE**

silence, stillness, calmness

(adjective)
# PREDESTINARIAN

## MEANING

Believing things are determined by fate.

## EXAMPLE

The grandfather tried to explain his predestinarian beliefs to his grandson, but all the kid believed he was destined to do was win the video game he was playing on his phone.

## SIMILAR

preordained, predetermined

## OPPOSITE

free-willed, autonomous

(verb)

# exSANGUINATe

To drain blood.

I felt so bad for the newbie, inexperienced vampire who was unable to exsanguinate me that I made him a grilled cheese sandwich with tomato soup.

bleed, hemorrhage

replenish, infuse

(noun)

# HABITUE

---

Someone who visits a place often.

MEANING

---

## EXAMPLE

The pub's habitues were there so often that their wives didn't recognize their faces anymore.

## SIMILAR

a regular, patron

## OPPOSITE

stranger, newbie, transient

(adjective)

# BUMPTIOUS

MEANING

Being arrogant.

EXAMPLE

The bumptious customer bloviated a series of highfalutin words at me thinking I was an idiot, but I understood everything he said because I read "Big & Fancy Words".

SIMILAR

conceited, pretentious, cocky

OPPOSITE

humble, reserved, shy

(noun)

# ONOMASTICS

The study of names.

MEANING

EXAMPLE

Harold Poop Balls was always curious about where his name came from, so he decided to dedicate his life to onomastics.

SIMILAR

etymology, toponymy

OPPOSITE

not the study of names

(noun)

# ADELPHOGAMY

A marriage between siblings.

Adelphogamy was quite common in the kingdom of Siblingonia, where the royal family believed in keeping the throne within the family tree – literally!

incest, sibling marriage

exogamy, endogamy

(noun)

# CLINOMANIA

MEANING

An excessive desire to stay in bed.

EXAMPLE

Tom's clinomania was so severe that he had to hire Larry to be his alarm clock and yell at him to get up.

SIMILAR

bed addiction, lethargy

OPPOSITE

morning person, early riser

(noun)

# MANORIALISM

A social and economic system in medieval Europe.

MEANING

EXAMPLE

Under the system of manorialism, a lord could take everything a peasant had, including their pot to pee in.

SIMILAR

feudalism, serfdom

OPPOSITE

capitalism, modernity

**JUL 15**

(noun)

# BeLONePHOBIA

An extreme fear of needles or sharp objects.

Jerry's belonephobia was so severe that he once faked having diarrhea to avoid getting a flu shot at the doctor's office!

trypanophobia, aichmophobia

acupuncture love, fearlessness

(verb)

# GONGOOZLE

To stare idly or leisurely MEANING at something.

Jackson loved to gongoozle at the ducks swimming in the canal, but he often forgot to pay attention to where he was walking and ended up falling in.

SIMILAR

gawk, observe casually

OPPOSITE

ignore, overlook

# LASSITUDE
(noun)

MEANING

A lack of physical or mental energy.

EXAMPLE

Karen was always under a cloud of lassitude because of her endless complaining to the manager.

SIMILAR

fatigue, tiredness, exhaustion

OPPOSITE

strength, vigor, vim

(noun)

# IMPERMEABILIZATION

The process of making something resistant to the penetration of fluids. MEANING

EXAMPLE

After the 'impermeabilization' of the chocolate fountain, no one had to worry about accidental chocolate rain showers at the party!

SIMILAR

waterproofing, sealing

OPPOSITE

permeability, leakage

(noun)

# CICATRIZ

## A scar.

Mark tattooed around his cicatriz so cleverly that it actually looked like a cat's backside instead of an awful scar.

## mark, blemish

## smoothness, clarity

(adjective)

# RUPICOLOUS

Referring to plants or animals that live or grow on MEANING rocks.

EXAMPLE

The rupicolous goats in the mountains are like expert climbers, turning cliffs into their very own playgrounds!

SIMILAR

saxicolous, lithophilous

OPPOSITE

hydrophilous, xerophilous

(adjective)

# nUDIUSTErTIAN

## MEANING

Pertaining to the day before yesterday.

## EXAMPLE

Harry's nudiustertian excuse for missing the meeting was that he accidentally invented a time machine and got stuck in the past.

## SIMILAR

day-before-yesterday, pre-yesterday

## OPPOSITE

tomorrow, future

(adjective)

# OPALESCENT

Showing of many colors.

After eating strawberry ice cream, cotton candy, and corn dogs and then riding the roller coaster, Dan's projectile vomit looked like an opalescent double rainbow.

colorful, lustrous, vibrant

dull, plain, matte

(verb)

# PROSELYTIZE

To convert someone to your ideas.

When his wife tried to proselytize him into becoming a good listener, his response was always "Yes, dear.".

advocate, preach, brainwash

oppose, discourage

(noun)

# PATRICIAN

A person of high-class society.

MEANING

EXAMPLE

After reading the entire "Big & Fancy Words" vocabulary book, he could converse with some of the most brilliant patricians of our time.

SIMILAR

elite, noble, aristocrat

OPPOSITE

commoner, low-life

# XERTZ  (verb)

To gulp down or swallow quickly and eagerly.

After a long hike, Mandy xertzed her energy drink so fast that the blue liquid started coming out of her nose and ears.

chug, guzzle

Sip, savor

(noun)

# Gnossienne

A type of unconventional
musical composition.

MEANING

EXAMPLE

The gnossienne played by the piano
prodigy had such a calming effect that
it put the audience into a deep sleep,
resulting in a snoring symphony.

SIMILAR

musical piece, composition

OPPOSITE

discordant noise, dissonant cacophony

(noun)

# NURDLe

A small, rounded piece or plastic fragment.

The beachcomber found a nurdle so tiny that even the seagulls mistook it for a gourmet fish egg and started fighting over it.

fragment, particle

whole, intact object

(noun)

# TYROTOXISM

Poisoning caused by the consumption of dairy products.

After devouring a carton of expired yogurt, Shelly had a case of tyrotoxism and developed an unexpected talent for singing in the key of "moos."

dairy poisoning, milk toxification

dairy safety, lactose tolerance

(noun)

# CONFUTATION

The act of proving someone wrong.

Tom's confutation of Mia's theory that pigs can not fly was so believable, he had the whole office looking out the windows.

disproof, rebuttal

validation, conformation

(noun)

# DAMOZEL

A young, single woman.

MEANING

EXAMPLE

The playful damozel taunted all the single men of the village with her extremely large feet and enormous forehead which was the standard of beauty at the time.

SIMILAR

damsel, maiden

OPPOSITE

wife, married woman, matron

(verb)

# IMPIGNORATE

## MEANING

To pledge something as collateral for a debt.

## EXAMPLE

In a desperate attempt to buy a lifetime supply of glitter, Ryan impignorated his collection of rare clown shoes, leaving him with nothing but big-footed regrets.

## SIMILAR

mortgage, pawn

## OPPOSITE

redeem, reclaim

# QUIRE

(noun)

A unit of measurement for paper, typically equal to 24 or 25 sheets.

MEANING

EXAMPLE

Lisa's obsession with stationery reached new heights when she used an entire quire of paper to write a single sentence: "I love glittery pens!"

SIMILAR

ream, bundle

OPPOSITE

sheet, individual paper

(adjective)

# QUADRATOMANDIBULAR

Referring to something absurdly complex.

The professor's quadratomandibular explanation of time travel left the students more confused than a chicken trying to understand quantum physics.

ultra-complicated, hyper-elaborate

simple, straightforward

(verb)

# ULTRACREPIDATE

To give an opinion or criticize beyond one's area of expertise. MEANING

EXAMPLE

Despite being a self-proclaimed "pizza connoisseur," Randy ultracrepidated about the best way to launch rockets into space using pepperoni as fuel.

SIMILAR

overstep, exceed boundaries

OPPOSITE

stay in lane, respect limits

(noun)

# OBSECRATION

An urgent prayer or plea.

His obsecration for more ugly Christmas sweaters became so dramatic his mother asked him to seek help.

entreaty, supplication

command, refusal, declaration

(noun)

# POGONOTROPHY

The act of growing a
MEANING    beard.

EXAMPLE

After months of dedicated pogonotrophy, Grant's beard grew so long and unruly that birds started mistaking it for a luxurious bird condo.

SIMILAR

beard growth, facial hair cultivation

OPPOSITE

shaving, beard removal

(noun)

# THORACENTESIS

The removal of fluid from the chest. MEANING

EXAMPLE

Brian thought it would be funny to drink soda through his nose however, it turned tragic when he needed to get a thoracentesis to remove the liquid from his lungs.

SIMILAR

chest tap

OPPOSITE

injection of fluid, infusion

(noun)

# XEROPHTHALMIA

Dryness of the eyes.

MEANING

EXAMPLE

After spending hours staring at memes on his phone, Tracey experienced a brief bout of xerophthalmia, leading her to believe she had laughed her tears away.

SIMILAR

dry eye syndrome, keratoconjunctivitis Sicca

OPPOSITE

excessive tearing, hydrated eyes

# LETHOLOGICA (noun)

MEANING

The temporary inability to recall a specific word or name.

EXAMPLE

During the debate, Steven experienced a sudden case of lethologica and referred to the opposing candidate as "What's-his-face" for the rest of the evening.

SIMILAR

tip-of-the-tongue phenomenon, word-finding difficulty

OPPOSITE

perfect recall, fluent vocabulary

(adjective)

# ULOTRICHOUS

MEANING

Having woolly or tightly curled hair.

EXAMPLE

Albert's ulotrichous hairstyle was so voluminous that he would often store his wallet and a small lunch inside it.

SIMILAR

curly-haired, afro-textured

OPPOSITE

straight-haired, smooth-textured

(adjective)

# contumelious

Being arrogant and rude.

Jane's contumelious remarks at the fisherman's banquet were so insulting, even the shrimp cocktail got angry.

insulting, disdainful

nice, pleasant, respectful

(noun)
# KLUDGE

A makeshift solution or piece of equipment, for a temporary fix. MEANING

EXAMPLE

Tim's kludge to fix the leaky faucet involved duct-taping a rubber duck to the spout, resulting in a quirky but utterly inefficient bathroom experience.

SIMILAR

jury-rig, makeshift

OPPOSITE

professional fix, well-engineered solution

(noun/adjective)

# EMPYREAN

## MEANING

The highest heaven or celestial realm.

## EXAMPLE

The self-proclaimed "King of the Backyard" claimed his inflatable pool as his own personal empyrean, complete with floating beer holders and nacho boats.

## SIMILAR

heavenly, divine

## OPPOSITE

infernal, hellish

(noun)

# MELLILOT

A yellow-flowered plant or herb, often used as a culinary
MEANING ingredient.

EXAMPLE

Grandma's secret ingredient for her famous soup was a pinch of dried mellilot, which she claimed was a magic herb that made everyone believe they were republicans.

SIMILAR

herb, medicinal plant

OPPOSITE

inedible plant, toxic herb

(noun)

# AEROSOLIZATION

The process of converting a substance into tiny particles or MEANING droplets.

Vinny's attempt to impress his date with a self-aerosolization of cologne turned him into a human-shaped cloud, earning him the nickname 'Cologne-ius.'

SIMILAR

atomization, nebulization

OPPOSITE

condensation, solidification

(noun) # QUIDDITY

---

The essential nature or distinctive quality of something.

---

Philosopher Joe pondered the quiddity of socks and wondered why they had the uncanny ability to disappear, leaving behind a single lonely partner.

essence, nature

superficiality, insignificance

(adjective)
# EUPHONIOUS

MEANING

## Having a pleasant sound.

EXAMPLE

The chorus of singing toads in the swamp created an unexpected euphonious symphony that even the mosquitoes couldn't resist dancing to.

SIMILAR

melodious, harmonious

OPPOSITE

dissonant, cacophonous

(noun)

# VERBIGERATION

The repetition of words or phrases for no reason.

At the stand-up comedy show, the heckler's verbigeration of 'knock, knock' jokes got old fast, prompting the comedian to ask, 'Did you just escape a joke factory?'

echolalia (repetition of phrases), palilalia (repetition of one's own words)

eloquence, varied speech

# AGELAST (noun)

A person who never laughs or finds anything funny.

MEANING

EXAMPLE

Tom, the self-proclaimed agelast, remained stoic even when a clown fell into a bucket of spaghetti, causing an eruption of laughter from everyone else.

SIMILAR

unamused person, humorless individual

OPPOSITE

jovial person, laughter enthusiast

(noun)

# CHROMOLITHOGRAPH

A print or illustration produced using a multi-color printing process MEANING

EXAMPLE

Bill proudly displayed his new chromolithograph of a serene landscape, but his pet pigeon mistook it for a window and kept trying to fly through it.

SIMILAR

print, lithographic reproduction

OPPOSITE

monochrome sketch, black-and-white image

(verb)

# DELIQUESCE

MEANING

To dissolve or melt away into a liquid.

EXAMPLE

The forgotten ice cream cone deliquesced in the summer heat, leaving behind a sticky trail that led straight to a happy ant picnic.

SIMILAR

dissolve, liquefy

OPPOSITE

solidify, coagulate

# (noun) GLOAMING

The time of day between daylight and darkness; twilight.

MEANING

EXAMPLE

The mischievous elf preferred to conduct his pranks during the gloaming, as it provided just the right amount of mysterious ambiance to confuse the neighbors.

SIMILAR

dusk, twilight

OPPOSITE

daytime, noon

# HIRAETH (noun)

A feeling of homesickness or longing for a place that no longer exists or cannot be returned to.

MEANING

EXAMPLE

Stan experienced hiraeth for his childhood treehouse and tried to recreate it as an adult, only to realize that he had outgrown both the tree and the tiny door.

SIMILAR

nostalgia, longing

OPPOSITE

contentment, satisfaction

# INURE

(verb)

To become accustomed to something unpleasant.

After years of eating my mother's experimental meatloaf, the family had inured themselves to her creative combination of ingredients, including marshmallows, pickles, and potato chips.

accustom, habituate

sensitive, unprepared

(verb)

# PREPONDERATE

MEANING

## To dominate.

EXAMPLE

To preponderate his opponent in the ring, the wrestler gave him a wet willy while he had him in a headlock.

SIMILAR

prevail, outweigh, overtake

OPPOSITE

yield, submit, succumb

(noun)

# PETRICHOR

The pleasant, earthy smell that accompanies rain.

As the petrichor filled the air, the Venus Fly Traps rejoiced and began a synchronized dance routine, attracting a group of confused flies who soon became lunch.

earthy scent, rain smell

artificial scent, foul odor

(adjective)

# quiescent

In a state or period of inactivity or dormancy.

The couch potato's quiescent lifestyle was interrupted only by occasional outbreaks of chip-crunching and sporadic laughter at cheesy late-night infomercials.

dormant, inactive

active, lively

(adjective)

# INEQUIGRANULAR

Not uniform or consistent in grain size. MEANING

EXAMPLE

Trying to make toast with inequigranular yeast extract was like spreading huge rocks on bread!

SIMILAR

nonuniform, heterogeneous

OPPOSITE

uniform, homogeneous

# AUG 28

# QUERENCIA

A place or source of comfort, where one feels safe.

MEANING

EXAMPLE

For Ernie, the local doughnut shop was his querencia, where he sought solace and reassurance from the warm embrace of glazed yumminess.

SIMILAR

safe haven, comfort zone

OPPOSITE

unfamiliar territory, discomfort

# CYNOSURE (noun)

MEANING

A person or thing that is the center of attention.

EXAMPLE

The chatty boy, equipped with a top hat and singing talent, became the cynosure of the neighborhood, attracting a group of enthusiastic but tone-deaf fans.

SIMILAR

center of attention, spotlight

OPPOSITE

inconspicuous, unnoticed

(noun)

# BASIOPHTHALMITE

A fossilized eye socket of an ancient organism.

The archaeologist was ecstatic to find a perfectly preserved basiophthalmite, but the rest of the team couldn't understand why he was so excited about an old eyeball holder.

eye socket fossil, ocular orbitite

living eye socket, modern orbit structure

(noun)

# NYMPHOLEPSY

An intense infatuation with young, beautiful women or a passionate enthusiasm for the MEANING natural world.

EXAMPLE

Ever since he read that fantasy book with forest nymphs, Brad developed a severe case of nympholepsy, spending weekends in the woods with his binoculars, hoping to spot one.

SIMILAR

nymphomania, nature-lover's ecstasy

OPPOSITE

disinterest, apathy

# PALINDROME

(noun)

A word or phrase that reads the same forward as it does backward.

MEANING

EXAMPLE

"Yo, banana boy," Hannah yelled to the banana seller, "Do you know what a palindrome is?".
"I do now!" said the boy.

SIMILAR

mirror word, reversible phrase

OPPOSITE

asymmetrical word

(noun)

# WHEREWITHAL

MEANING

The means or resources to accomplish something.

EXAMPLE

John never found the wherewithal to stand up to the bully, resulting in daily wedgies all throughout middle school.

SIMILAR

resources, capability

OPPOSITE

lack, insufficiency

(noun)

# FeLonious

Something that is related to or characteristic of a crime.

The dog's felonious attempt to steal all the cookies from the kitchen jar ended with him caught red-pawed by the household cat, who promptly called the authorities.

criminal, unlawful

innocent, lawful

(adjective)

# SERIOCOMIC

MEANING

Describes something with comic
and serious elements.

EXAMPLE

Tony's will was very seriocomic
because he asked that at his
funeral he be dressed like a clown
and his body shot out of a cannon
into the grave.

SIMILAR tragic comedy

OPPOSITE

not serious or comical

(noun)

# DEMONOLOGY

The study or belief in demons, their nature, characteristics, powers, and how they interact with humans and the supernatural realm.    MEANING

EXAMPLE

Sean decided to enroll in a demonology course, hoping it would help him deal with his unruly neighbors, but he quickly realized it wasn't teaching him how to summon a 'demon of peace and quiet.'

SIMILAR

occultism, diabolism

OPPOSITE

angelology (the study of angels), theology (the study of deities or gods)

(adjective)

# LOTOPHAGOUS

MEANING

Describes someone or something that eats a lot of lotus or any substance that induces a dreamy or lethargic state.

EXAMPLE

After binge-watching an entire series on the weekend, Christy felt lotophagous, as if she had absorbed the fictional world into her very being.

SIMILAR

lethargic, dreamy

OPPOSITE

energetic, alert

(adjective)

# PERSPICACIOUS

Having keen mental perception and understanding.

MEANING

EXAMPLE

Despite his glasses, the perspicacious robot couldn't find his way out of the library.

SIMILAR

insightful, astute

OPPOSITE

obtuse, unaware

(noun)

# VERISIMILITUDE

The appearance or semblance of truth; the quality of

MEANING being realistic.

EXAMPLE

The actor's fake mustache added an extra touch of verisimilitude to his character.

SIMILAR

authenticity, plausibility

OPPOSITE

falseness, fabrication

(noun)

# ACCOUTREMENT

Additional items or accessories associated with a particular activity or style. MEANING

EXAMPLE

The chef's kitchen had all the necessary accoutrements, including knives, ovens, and an in-house psychiatrist.

SIMILAR

equipment, paraphernalia

OPPOSITE

bareness, minimalism

(noun)

# ICHTHYOLOGY

MEANING

## The study of fish.

EXAMPLE

When the ichthyology professor accidentally dropped her cheeseburger into the piranha tank during a lecture, the fish had a feast while the students had a laugh.

SIMILAR

fishology, pisces science

OPPOSITE

ornithology (study of birds), mammalogy (study of mammals)

(noun)

# LIPOGRAMMATIST

A person who writes the text of a group of letters where a vowel or consonant is consistently omitted. MEANING

EXAMPLE

The aspiring lipogrammatist attempted to write a story without using the letter 'E,' but it soon became a saga of absurd substitutions and quirky synonyms.

SIMILAR

language experimenter, word game enthusiast

OPPOSITE

verbose writer, letter-lavish author

(noun)

# KINETOGENESIS

The generation or production of motion or movement.

Allen's attempt at kinetogenesis using a homemade rocket ended up with him flying like a bird – straight into a dumpster.

motion generation, movement production

stagnation, immobility

(verb)

# BOMBINATE

To make a buzzing or humming noise.

*MEANING*

*EXAMPLE*

The metal chair bombinated when Clark farted.

*SIMILAR*

buzz, drone

*OPPOSITE*

silence, stillness

(adjective)
# CATADIOPTRIC

## MEANING

Referring to an optical system that combines both lenses and mirrors to reflect light.

## EXAMPLE

After assembling his catadioptric telescope backward, Jerry ended up observing his neighbor's living room instead of the stars, which led to some awkward eye contact.

## SIMILAR

reflective-refractive, compound optical

## OPPOSITE

monocular (using a single lens), refractive-only

(noun)

# INTEROSCULATION

The act of connecting or joining together.

MEANING

EXAMPLE

The gardening club's attempt at creating a hedge maze turned into a tangled mess of interosculation, leaving visitors more lost than a chicken with no head.

SIMILAR

confluence, fusion

OPPOSITE

separation, disconnection

# GAMBOL (verb)

MEANING

## To run or jump about playfully.

EXAMPLE

The children gambolled down the hill so enthusiastically that they all tripped and face-planted in the dirt.

SIMILAR

frolic, romp

OPPOSITE

rest, stillness

# SEP 17

(noun)

# HELIOLATRY

Worship or excessive admiration of the sun.

MEANING

EXAMPLE

Ancient civilizations often practiced heliolatry which turned their skin into what resembled a old leather wallet.

SIMILAR

sun worship, solar reverence

OPPOSITE

heliophobia, sun aversion

(verb)

# OBNUBILATE

To obscure or cloud something.

The dense fog obnubilated the view, making it impossible to see the elephants mating.

hide, veil

clarify, reveal

(noun)

# HYPOPHRENIA

A mental condition characterized by low intelligence, dullness, or cognitive impairment.

MEANING

EXAMPLE

When the teacher asked if anyone had questions, Mia raised her hand and asked, 'Is hypophrenia contagious? Because I think I might have caught it from my friend.'

SIMILAR

mental impairment, cognitive deficiency

OPPOSITE

high intelligence, sharpness

# BELLICOSE (adjective)

Inclined to start quarrels or engage in warfare.

MEANING

EXAMPLE

The bellicose student would always start a fight with his classmates by flicking snots at them.

SIMILAR

aggressive, belligerent

OPPOSITE

peaceful, pacifistic

(adjective)

# VEXATIOUS

Causing annoyance or distress.

The constant nagging of my wife was vexatious, preventing me from falling asleep.

irritating, bothersome

pleasant, soothing

(adjective) # BALeFUL

## MEANING

Threatening harm or evil.

## EXAMPLE

The witch cast a baleful glance at the villagers making several of them crap their pants.

## SIMILAR

menacing, sinister

## OPPOSITE

benign, harmless

(noun)

# OPACIMETER

A device used to measure the opacity of a liquid or gas.

EXAMPLE

When the scientist tried to use the opacimeter, the machine just sneezed and said, 'Sorry, I'm allergic to dust, can we measure something else?'

SIMILAR

turbidimeter, haze meter

OPPOSITE

transparent meter, clarity gauge

(adjective)

# INDEFATIGABLE

## Tireless or persisting

MEANING **tirelessly.**

EXAMPLE

The indefatigable whimpering of the old Shih Tzu made its owner so crazy he jumped out the second-floor window.

SIMILAR

**unflagging, unwavering**

OPPOSITE

exhausted, weary

(adjective)

# JeJune

Dull, lacking interest or significance. MEANING

EXAMPLE

The students' jejune book reports were so bland, that the teacher fell asleep with his head in his morning granola.

SIMILAR

insipid, vapid

OPPOSITE

stimulating, engaging

(noun)

# TREDECILLION

## MEANING

A very large numerical value equal to 1 followed by 42 zeros.

## EXAMPLE

When asked how much he loved ice cream, Chris replied, 'I love it a tredecillion times more than all the socks I've lost in the dryer!'

## SIMILAR

quintillion, sextillion

## OPPOSITE

thousand, million

(adjective)

# LABYRINTHINE

Intricate and confusing,
like a labyrinth.

MEANING

EXAMPLE

Navigating through the labyrinthine corridors of the mansion proved to be a challenge so the rich man left hundred dollar bills on the ground to find his way back.

SIMILAR

complicated, convoluted

OPPOSITE

direct, straightforward

(adjective)

# MAGNANIMOUS

Generous and forgiving, especially towards a rival or enemy.

MEANING

EXAMPLE

Despite the harsh criticism, she responded with a magnanimous gesture, offering to make her enemy a vanilla milkshake.

SIMILAR

generous, noble

OPPOSITE

vindictive, petty

(adjective)

# QUOTIDIAN

Occurring or experienced daily.

MEANING

EXAMPLE

Her morning routine included the quotidian tasks of brushing her teeth and yelling "I love frogs" three times.

SIMILAR

daily, routine

OPPOSITE

occasional, sporadic

(verb)

# TRANSMOGRIFY

## MEANING

To completely transform or change in appearance or form.

## EXAMPLE

The magician's spell caused the rabbit to transmogrify into a hot dog and then he ate it.

## SIMILAR

metamorphose, mutate

## OPPOSITE

preserve, maintain

(adjective)

# SEMPITERNAL

Eternal, everlasting, or enduring forever. MEANING

EXAMPLE

The sempiternal debate over pineapple on pizza continued unabated, with no resolution in sight, leading some to believe it was a timeless cosmic dilemma.

SIMILAR

eternal, timeless

OPPOSITE

temporary, fleeting

(noun)

# CATAPLEXY

Sudden loss of muscle control triggered by strong MEANING emotions.

When I heard the corny joke, I experienced cataplexy and collapsed like a deflated balloon.

SIMILAR

narcolepsy, sleep paralysis

OPPOSITE

alertness, vigilance

# OCT 3

# NOCTILUCENT

Emitting light or glowing
during the night or twilight
hours. MEANING

EXAMPLE

The noctilucent mushrooms in the
garden glowed so brightly that the
fireflies organized a rave party around
them, complete with tiny disco balls and
electric bug music.

SIMILAR

luminescent, phosphorescent

OPPOSITE

dark, non-glowing

(noun)

# COGITATION

The process of thinking deeply.

MEANING

EXAMPLE

After much cogitation, Shanon decided to go with the one green sock with the one red sock even though it was Halloween.

reflection, contemplation SIMILAR

OPPOSITE

impulsive, indifferent

(noun/adjective)

# SAPIOSEXUAL

A person who finds intelligence or mental stimulation sexually attractive. MEANING

EXAMPLE

Jenny's online dating profile stated that she was sapiosexual, which led to many suitors sending her love poems in binary code and complicated math equations.

SIMILAR

intellectually attracted, brainy preference

OPPOSITE

aversion to intelligence, shallow attraction

(adjective)

# ZENITHAL

Relating to or situated at the highest point; directly above or overhead.

Larry's break dance performance reached the zenithal of hilarity when he spun on his head and accidentally kicked the chicken into the chocolate fountain.

highest, apex

lowest, nadir

(adjective)

# HALCYON

Calm, peaceful, and carefree; denoting a period of tranquility. MEANING

EXAMPLE

The halcyon beach vacation turned chaotic when Uncle Fred mistook the sandcastle for a giant ice cream cone and attracted an army of seagulls.

SIMILAR

serene, tranquil

OPPOSITE

turbulent, chaotic

(adjective)

# SOLIVAGANT

MEANING

## Wandering alone in solitary journeys.

EXAMPLE

John's solivagant adventures through the grocery store led to multiple conspiracy theories about why he always ended up in the pickle aisle.

SIMILAR

wanderer, lone traveler

OPPOSITE

group traveler, accompanied wanderer

(noun)

# LIMERENCE

The state of being obsessed

with someone. MEANING

EXAMPLE

Tim's limerence for the pizza delivery person reached such heights that he composed a sonnet to declare his love, complete with pepperoni metaphors and cheese similes.

SIMILAR

infatuation, obsession

OPPOSITE

apathy, indifference

(noun)

# QUADRUMVIRATE

A group of four individuals who collaborate or work together.

The quadrumvirate of friends decided to form a secret club, but it quickly fell apart when they couldn't agree on the club's name, motto, or whether to have a secret handshake.

quartet, fourfold alliance

solo, individuality

(noun)

# SOMNAMBULIST

A person who sleepwalks.

MEANING

EXAMPLE

Sally, the somnambulist extraordinaire, once sleepwalked into the kitchen and made a gourmet sandwich masterpiece, only to wake up and find mustard in her slippers.

SIMILAR

sleepwalker, noctambulist

OPPOSITE

wakeful person, insomniac

(noun)

# DACTYLION

## MEANING

The tip of the middle finger or the center of the palm.

## EXAMPLE

Using his dactylion as a magic wand, Blane attempted to turn his pet turtle into a pizza but accidentally transformed himself into a beach ball instead.

## SIMILAR

fingertip, palm center

## OPPOSITE

elbow, knee

(noun/verb)

# TINCTURE

A slight coloring, flavor, or trace of something.   MEANING

EXAMPLE

Grandpa's soup had a tincture of magic that turned anyone who tasted it into a singing unicorn, much to the surprise of my band during our weekly rehearsal.

SIMILAR

flavoring, hint

OPPOSITE

removal, extraction

(adjective)

# RETICENT

Inclined to be silent, reserved, or hesitant in speech.

MEANING

EXAMPLE

Frank, the reticent ventriloquist, had a puppet that spoke in rhymes, but he himself couldn't utter a single word without tripping over his own tongue.

SIMILAR

reserved, quiet

OPPOSITE

talkative, outgoing

# OCT 15

(adjective)

# TREMULOUS

Shaking or trembling slightly due to nervousness or fear. MEANING

The tremulous toddler's dance moves were so enthusiastic that they caused a miniature earthquake, leading the family cat to question the stability of the house.

quivering, shaky

steady, stable

(adjective) # XERIC

Dry or characterized by a lack of moisture.

Jerry's attempt at creating a xeric rainforest in his backyard using a single cactus and a water pistol led to some very confused and dehydrated birds.

dry, arid

wet, humid

(adjective)

# DISCORDANT

Lacking harmony or agreement. MEANING

EXAMPLE

The cat and dog duet was so discordant that the neighborhood birds formed a protest choir, demanding the return of their solace.

SIMILAR

dissonant, clashing

OPPOSITE

harmonious, melodious

(adjective)

# HERMETIC

Airtight or sealed in a way that prevents the entry or escape of air.

Cheri's hermetic pickle jar was so impenetrable that even the most skilled pickle thieves couldn't access the crunchy treasures within.

airtight, sealed

open, permeable

# OCT 19

(adjective)

# INCIPIENT

In an early stage of development. MEANING

EXAMPLE

Henry's incipient talent for juggling flaming bowling balls resulted in a memorable family picnic when the bowling balls became fiery meteors chasing after the potato salad.

SIMILAR

beginning, initial

OPPOSITE

mature, fully developed

(adjective) # RUBICUND

## Having a healthy, reddish complexion.

After spending an hour under the hot sun, My attempt at achieving a rubicund complexion turned me into a walking tomato, complete with tomato-scented cologne.

rosy, flushed

pale, pallid

(adjective)

# DIGONOPOROUS

Referring to a plant or organism that has two openings or pores.

MEANING

EXAMPLE

The biologists were delighted to discover a new species of plant that was digonoporous, but they couldn't agree on what to name it, so they ended up calling it 'Confusedus Flora.'

SIMILAR

bizonoporous (having two pores), duplex-porous

OPPOSITE

monoporous (having one pore), aporous (lacking pores)

(noun)

# EQUANIMITY

Mental calmness, composure, or evenness of temper.

MEANING

EXAMPLE

Despite being chased by a horde of angry geese, Ron maintained his equanimity by reciting soothing lullabies, causing the geese to fall asleep mid-honk.

SIMILAR

composure, serenity

OPPOSITE

panic, agitation

(noun)

# GROBIAN

A rude person.

At dinner Billy revealed how much of a grobian he was by picking everything from his nose to his teeth to his naval to his seat.

ruffian, unsophisticated person

a polite person, a nice person

(adjective)

# INTRANSIGENT

MEANING

Unwilling or refusing to change one's views, beliefs, or course of action; stubbornly resistant.

EXAMPLE

Despite overwhelming evidence and a parade of experts, the intransigent mime refused to break character, leaving the jury confused and the judge lost for words.

SIMILAR

stubborn, uncompromising

OPPOSITE

flexible, adaptable

(adjective)

# ICTERITIOUS

Having a yellowish color, usually on the skin.   MEANING

EXAMPLE

The icteritious hue of Jane's skin was caused by eating only blueberries and grasshoppers for three weeks straight.

SIMILAR

jaundiced, yellowish

OPPOSITE

rosy, bluish

(noun)

# PASTOPHORIUM

MEANING A small chamber or room in an ancient temple or church.

EXAMPLE

When Donny accidentally locked himself in the pastophorium, he tried to pray for divine intervention, but all he got was an echo of his own voice talking to sacred robes.

SIMILAR

sacristy, vestry

OPPOSITE

sanctuary (main sacred area of a church), atrium (open central space of a building)

(adjective/noun)

# SOPORIFIC

A medication that promotes sleep. MEANING

EXAMPLE

The soporific lullaby sung by the mother was so effective that the whole neighborhood decided to hire her as the official bedtime singer, resulting in a boost in local sleep quality.

SIMILAR

sleep-inducing, somnolent

OPPOSITE

stimulating, energizing

(adjective) # TENEBROUS

## MEANING

Dark, shadowy, or obscure in nature.

## EXAMPLE

Mark's tenebrous basement became the perfect breeding ground for his collection of glow-in-the-dark monkeys, creating a mesmerizing but slightly eerie jungle in the depths.

## SIMILAR

dark, shadowy

## OPPOSITE

bright, illuminated

(verb)

# LYOPHILIZE

## To freeze dry.

Lily attempted to lyophilize her leftover pizza, hoping it would last forever, but all she got was a crispy, unappetizing slice of 'astronaut food.'

dehydrate, desiccate

rehydrate (to add water back),
saturate (to fully soak with liquid)

(noun)

# VEXILLOLOGY

## The study of flags.

When Jared became bored of stamp collecting, he moved on to vexillology, cementing his place in the NERD HALL OF FAME.

heraldry, vexillography

flag ignorance

(noun)

# IMPRECATION

A spoken curse.

MEANING

EXAMPLE

The old witch muttered an imprecation at the kids, wishing them never to be able to eat candy ever again. It didn't work!

SIMILAR

a wish of misfortune

OPPOSITE

prayer, blessing

# WELTER (noun)

A state of confusion or disorder.

In the aftermath of the storm, a welter of debris was stuck in my hair.

chaos, turmoil

order, organization

**NOV 2**

(noun)

# APHELION

The point in the orbit of a planet that is farthest from the MEANING sun.

EXAMPLE

When the Earth is in aphelion, my nipples get hard.

SIMILAR

farthest point, apogee

OPPOSITE

perihelion, closest point

(adjective)

# EXTEMPORANEOUS

Done without

preparation or on

MEANING the spot.

EXAMPLE

The comedian's extemporaneous
jokes had the audience blowing beer
out of their noses.

SIMILAR

impromptu, spontaneous

OPPOSITE

rehearsed, planned

(noun)

# ANATHEMA

Something or someone that is intensely disliked. MEANING

EXAMPLE

Attempting to wear socks with sandals in our fashion-forward office was deemed an anathema by the style police.

SIMILAR

abomination, abhorrence

OPPOSITE

beloved, cherished

(noun)

# ALLUVION

A buildup of sediment from flowing water.

## EXAMPLE

His bathroom was so dirty that when his toilet overflowed, it created a modern art alluvion in the corner.

## SIMILAR

dirt deposit, silt mound

## OPPOSITE

erosion, depletion

(noun)

# FLIBBERTIGIBBET

A frivolous or flighty person.

MEANING

EXAMPLE

She's a flibbertigibbet, she gives me a headache always jumping from one topic to another without pausing for breath.

SIMILAR

scatterbrain, chatterbox

OPPOSITE

serious, focused

(noun)

# EREMITE

A person who lives in seclusion.

When Jenny's friends invited her to a wild party, she declined, claiming she had embraced her inner eremite and preferred the company of her pet rock over social gatherings.

recluse, anchorite

Socialite (someone who enjoys socializing), extrovert

# NOV 8

(noun)

# LIMNOLOGY

The study of inland waters, such as lakes, ponds, and rivers.

When Todd told his friends he was studying limnology, they thought he was researching limos, and he had to explain that he'd rather explore lakes than luxury cars.

hydrology (study of water), aquatic ecology

terrestrial biology (study of land-based organisms), oceanography (study of oceans)

(noun)

# ALIENICOLA

An organism that lives in a habitat that is foreign or alien to it.

MEANING

EXAMPLE

The penguin felt like quite the alienicola when it accidentally waddled into a seagull party on the beach in Florida.

SIMILAR

xenophile (one attracted to foreign things), non-native

OPPOSITE

autochthonous (originating from the same habitat), Native

(noun)

# PARVANIMITY

A lack of generosity.

When it came to sharing snacks, Jim's parvanimity was evident as he claimed he could only part with one chip per person.

stinginess, petiteness

generosity, magnanimity

(adjective)

# UXORIOUS

Excessively fond or submissive to one's wife.

*MEANING*

*EXAMPLE*

John was so uxorious that he would do anything his wife asked, even if it meant wearing matching duck outfits.

*SIMILAR*

submissive, devoted

*OPPOSITE*

independent, assertive

(verb)

# ABSQUATULATE

To leave abruptly or

MEANING secretly.

EXAMPLE

When the bill arrived, he absquatulated, leaving his friends to cover the expenses.

SIMILAR

depart, flee

OPPOSITE

arrive, stay

(noun)

# BIBLIOPOLE

## MEANING

A seller or collector of books.

## EXAMPLE

The bibliopole's personal library contained rare and valuable books about taxidermy.

## SIMILAR

bookseller, book collector

## OPPOSITE

bibliophobe, book-lover

(noun)

# zoonosis

A disease that can be transmitted between animals and humans. MEANING

EXAMPLE

The doctor told me it was zoonosis caused by kissing that monkey.

SIMILAR

animal-borne disease, cross-species infection

OPPOSITE

human-only, non-transmissible

(adjective)

# BRUMOUS

## Misty or foggy.

The brumous weather made it difficult to see but it looked like seven or eight clowns were riding a motorcycle.

foggy, hazy

clear, sunny

(adverb)

# VIDELICET

Something that follows.
"That is to say...".

MEANING

EXAMPLE

Sean loves taxidermy-
videlicet, stuffed penguins
and stuffed toads.

SIMILAR

namely, specifically

OPPOSITE

vaguely, genuinely, broadly

(adjective)

# FOUDROYANT

MEANING

## Overwhelmingly impressive or stunning.

EXAMPLE

The actor's foudroyant performance in playing the part of a tree left the audience with their jaws on the ground.

SIMILAR

astonishing, dazzling

OPPOSITE

underwhelming, unimpressive

(noun)

# GARGALESTHESIA

The sensation caused by tickling. MEANING

EXAMPLE

After the dog licked her feet she experienced a delightful bout of gargalesthesia.

SIMILAR

ticklishness, tickle response

OPPOSITE

numbness, insensitivity

(noun)

# ZOANTHROPY

The delusion of being

MEANING an animal.

EXAMPLE

He believed he was a donkey and would often walk around on all fours braying, a clear case of zoanthropy.

SIMILAR

animal delusion, species identity disorder

OPPOSITE

human, humanoid

(adjective)

# IMPAVID

Fearless or undaunted.

*MEANING*

*EXAMPLE*

Despite the haunted house's reputation, he entered it impavidly, but soon became frightened when a ghost offered him pie.

*SIMILAR*

brave, courageous

*OPPOSITE*

fearful, timid

(adjective)

# CECIDOGENOUS

MEANING

An abnormal outgrowth on a plant.

EXAMPLE

Sandra's eccentric fashion sense included wearing cecidogenous accessories like earrings made from tiny plant galls, prompting people to call her the 'Gall Queen'.

SIMILAR

gall-inducing, gall-forming

OPPOSITE

non-gall, normal

(noun)

# KAKORRHAPHIOPHOBIA

The fear of failure or defeat.   MEANING

EXAMPLE

His kakorrhaphiophobia was so severe that he would start sweating just at the sight of a mini-golf course.

SIMILAR

atychiphobia, fear of failure

OPPOSITE

fearlessness, confidence

(noun)

# OMPHALOSKEPSIS

Contemplation of one's navel as an aid to self-reflection.

MEANING

EXAMPLE

During her omphaloskepsis, she pondered the meaning of life and her place in the universe, and also found a ball of lint.

SIMILAR

navel-gazing, self-reflection

OPPOSITE

external focus, engagement with others

# NOV 24

(verb)

# QUOMODOCUNQUIZE

MEANING

## To make money by any means possible.

He was willing to quomodocunquize, even if it meant engaging in the unethical practice of lizard racing.

SIMILAR

money-grub, profit-seek

OPPOSITE

content, satisfied

(adjective) **RIDENT**

*MEANING*

# Inclined to smile or laugh.

*EXAMPLE*

Her rident personality brightened up the room, even though she had spinach in her teeth.

*SIMILAR*

smiling, jovial

*OPPOSITE*

serious, gloomy

(noun)

# SABAISM

The worship of stars or celestial objects.

*MEANING*

*EXAMPLE*

Ancient cultures practiced sabaism praying to the stars for candy bars.

*SIMILAR*

star worship, celestial reverence

*OPPOSITE*

monotheism, atheism

(noun)

# TRISKELION

A symbol or design with three interlocking

spirals.

When Bob tried to impress his friends with his new dance move called the 'Triskelion Twist,' they all ended up in a tangle of limbs and laughter.

triple spiral, three-legged symbol

static, immobile

(adjective)

# BATHYKOLPIAN

Having ample breasts.

Her bathykolpian figure caused a problem when she ran, always leaving her with two black eyes.

full-bosomed, curvaceous

flat-chested, small-breasted

(adjective)

# APHRODISIAN

MEANING

Pertaining to love or desire, especially of a sexual nature.

EXAMPLE

After consuming the so-called 'Aphrodisian Smoothie,' Ted found himself flirting not only with humans but also with plants, convinced he had developed a love connection with a venus fly trap.

SIMILAR

erotic, sensual

OPPOSITE

chaste, platonic

(noun)

# CACOMISTLE

A small, nocturnal mammal native to North America.

MEANING

EXAMPLE

When the cacomistle spotted a group of tourists, it thought, 'Time to show off my acrobatic skills!' and attempted an elaborate somersault, only to land in a heap of its own poop.

SIMILAR

ringtail, bassarisk

OPPOSITE

desynchronize, unsynchronize

(verb)

# DIPHTHONGIZE

To form or pronounce as a diphthong.

MEANING

EXAMPLE

In some dialects, speakers diphthongize certain vowel sounds, causing them to attract the interest of the local platypus community.

SIMILAR

vowel blend, sound modification

OPPOSITE

combine - separate

(noun)

# EXSIBILATION

The act of booing,

MEANING

or hissing.

EXAMPLE

The comedian's offensive jokes about bananas were met with exsibilation from the audience.

SIMILAR

booing, catcalling

OPPOSITE

applause, cheering

(adjective)

# GADARENE

## MEANING

Recklessly or hastily advancing.

## EXAMPLE

In a gadarene fashion, he rushed into the cave only to emerge covered in bat poop.

## SIMILAR

impulsive, heedless

## OPPOSITE

cautious, deliberate

(noun)

# FISSILINGUAL

Having a split or forked tongue. MEANING

EXAMPLE

Some people are fissilingual, surgically slicing their tongues because they want to become reptiles.

SIMILAR

Bifurcated tongue, forked tongue

OPPOSITE

open, closed

(adjective)

# HIPPOCREPIAN

Pertaining to horses or resembling a

MEANING horse.

EXAMPLE

His wife had a hippocrepian face, which made her very popular at the jockey party.

SIMILAR

equine, horse-like

OPPOSITE

light, heavy

(noun)

# OSCITATION

The act of yawning.

MEANING

EXAMPLE

Stan's oscitation at the lecture on quasars was so dramatic you could see his fillings from space.

SIMILAR

drowsiness, boredom

OPPOSITE

alertness, wakefulness

(adjective)

# JUGLANDACEOUS

## MEANING

Having characteristics of walnut trees.

## EXAMPLE

The juglandaceous aroma of freshly baked walnut bread affected my nut allergies causing my face to turn purple.

## SIMILAR

walnut-like, nutty

## OPPOSITE

non-nutty, non-walnut-like

(noun)

# KTENOLOGY

The science of putting people to death.

He studied ktenology to help flies with nut allergies to relieve the pain with a peaceful death.

execution science, thanatology

life science, survival tactics

(adjective)

# LEPIDOPTEROLOGY

The scientific study of butterflies and moths.

Her passion for lepidopterology led her to develop strap-on butterfly wings which ended with a broken leg.

butterfly/moth study, lepidology

anti-butterfly/moth study, lepidophobia

(adjective)

# MeSONOXIAN

Pertaining to midnight or pertaining to a person who is MEANING active at night.

EXAMPLE

The mesonoxian musician rocked all night, and slept during the day.

SIMILAR

nocturnal, midnight-related

OPPOSITE

diurnal, daytime-related

(noun)

# NYCTOPHILIAC

MEANING

A person who loves the night.

EXAMPLE

As a nyctophiliac, she enjoyed stargazing while eating fried peanut butter and banana sandwiches.

SIMILAR

night lover, darkness enthusiast

OPPOSITE

hemerophile, day lover

(noun)

# OMBROPHOBIA

The fear or intense dislike
of rain. MEANING

EXAMPLE

His ombrophobia was so severe
that he always would hide
under cars with the first sound
of thunder.

SIMILAR

rain phobia, pluviophobia

OPPOSITE

pluviophilia, rain lover

(verb)

# QUAERITATE

To inquire or search for information.

I need to quaeritate the whereabouts of my mind.

inquire, investigate

ignore, disregard

# DEC 14

(noun)

# RHATHYMIA

An optimistic and cheerful
state of mind.

She faced each day with
rhathymia always smiling and
laughing to herself making her
seem crazy.

cheerfulness, optimism

depression, melancholy

(noun)

# SELACHOPHILE

A person who loves sharks.

The selachophile fell in love and got married to a hammerhead. They honeymooned at the Great Barrier Reef.

shark lover, shark enthusiast

selachophobe, shark hater

(adjective)

# TROGLODYTIC

Lacking in social skills or out of touch with the modern world. MEANING

EXAMPLE

His troglodytic habits included staying indoors all day with his blow-up doll wife that he ordered online.

SIMILAR

cave-like, hermit-like

OPPOSITE

sociable, modern

(adjective)

# inesculent

Not edible.

Tom's mashed potatoes were too inesculent for the dinner table but perfect to re-grout the bathroom tiles.

inedible, poison

palatable, tasty

(adjective)

# VULPINE

Resembling a fox.

MEANING

EXAMPLE

In his unique **vulpine** style, he once again tricked his sister into doing his chores including picking up the dog poop in the yard.

SIMILAR

fox-like, foxy

OPPOSITE

non-fox-like, non-cunning

(noun) # PARONOMASIA

A play on words.

MEANING

EXAMPLE

The old sea captain often relied on paronomasia, saying things like, "I'd rather have a bottle in front of me than a frontal lobotomy."

SIMILAR

pun, wordplay, witticism

OPPOSITE

literalism, direct speech

(adjective)

# LEPTODACTYLOUS

Having slender or thin fingers or toes.

*MEANING*

*EXAMPLE*

The frog's attempts at a high-five were always awkward due to its leptodactylous fingers, making it seem more like a jazz-hand enthusiast than a proper amphibian.

*SIMILAR*

slender-fingered, thin-toed

*OPPOSITE*

paddle-handed, stubby-toed

(noun) # ACNESTIS

The unreachable area of the back between the shoulder blades. MEANING

EXAMPLE

He struggled to scratch his acnestis and resorted to rubbing his back with a baguette.

SIMILAR

itchy spot, unreachable itch

OPPOSITE

reachable spot, accessible area

(noun)

# MENDICITY

The practice of begging.

The broke magician resorted to mendicity when trying to trade a magic trick for the last rabbit at the pet store during magic week.

panhandling, pauperism

wealth, prosperity

# DRUPELET (noun)

A small individual unit or segment of a compound fruit, such as a blackberry MEANING or raspberry.

The bird picked the berry drupelets out of Ted's long beard.

berry segment, fruitlet

whole fruit, non-segmented fruit

**DEC 24**

(noun)

# FELLMONGER

A person who buys/sells animal skins, and/or removes fur or wool from animals. MEANING

EXAMPLE

When Mary introduced her new boyfriend as a fellmonger, her friends couldn't help but make jokes about him having the 'hairiest' job in town.

SIMILAR

skinner, hide trader

OPPOSITE

vegan activist, animal rights advocate

(noun)

# GALIMATIAS

Confused or meaningless talk.

MEANING

Einstein's attempt to explain quantum physics to his dog resulted in a galimatias of barks, tail wags, and a very confused pup.

SIMILAR

gibberish, babble

OPPOSITE

clarity, coherence

(noun)

# HIRCISMUS

The odor or secretion of sweat from the armpits. MEANING

EXAMPLE

When Eric tried his new cologne, his attempt to attract attention resulted in unintended hircismus, making everyone wonder if a faint whiff of goat had suddenly taken an interest in fashion.

SIMILAR

armpit odor, underarm sweating

OPPOSITE

freshness, pleasant scent

(adjective)

# NECROPHAGOUS

MEANING

Refering to animals that feed on dead or decaying flesh.

EXAMPLE

Dana's attempts at cooking often resulted in dishes so unappetizing that even the neighborhood necrophagous ants gave them a wide berth.

SIMILAR

scavenging, carrion-eating

OPPOSITE

herbivorous (plant-eating), carnivorous (meat-eating)

(noun)

# KERAUNOGRAPH

A device used for recording or measuring thunder and lightning. MEANING

EXAMPLE

Ryan's homemade keraunograph, made with a lightning rod connected to a frying pan, cooked the most delicious crispy bacon.

SIMILAR

lightning recorder, thunder measuring device

OPPOSITE

non-lightning recorder, non-thunder measuring device

(noun)

# LALOCHEZIA

The relief or release gained by using vulgar or profane MEANING language.

EXAMPLE

She felt a momentary lalochezia when she stubbed her toe and let out a string of expletives.

SIMILAR

profanity relief, swearing catharsis

OPPOSITE

clean speech, non-vulgar expression

(noun)

# MUMPSIMUS

Person who stubbornly
adheres to a belief or
practice despite being shown
it is incorrect. MEANING

EXAMPLE

He is a mumpsimus who refuses to accept
that the Earth is round and revolves
around the Sun.

SIMILAR

stubborn believer, dogmatist

OPPOSITE

open-minded, adaptable

(noun)

# ARTOPHORION

A container for the Eucharist used in Catholic ceremonies.

MEANING

EXAMPLE

The congregation let out a huge gasp when Father Mulcahy's false teeth popped out and fell into the artophorion during mass.

SIMILAR

aedicule (small shrine or niche), shrine

OPPOSITE

open space, empty alcove

# ABOUT THE AUTHOR

ALBERT B. SQUID

If you spot this person please call our HOTLINE at 867-5309 ask for Tommy.

Born to a family of construction peeps, ALBERT B. SQUID was raised on construction sites in Massachusetts. Believe it or not, he holds two degrees in Engineering and Architecture and has worked as an Architect in Boston, Tokyo, and Seoul. In the year 2000, Squid started an independent children's book publishing company in NYC. I had fun doing that.....I mean HE (Albert B. Squid) had fun doing that! After becoming a freelance voice actor, the elusive author's whereabouts are unknown. He was last seen on a college campus in Amherst, Massachusetts talking about philosophy with a man named Mr. Black and his friend named Joe. He was heard asking "Where did my mind go?". To which Mr. Black replied "In the ocean." Kind of a strange conversation.

Did you find the humor of this book **sufficiently** edifying? If so you might also like the jocularity of its **predecessor**. Scan that QR to check it out!

albertbsquid.com

www.ingramcontent.com/pod-product-compliance
Lightning Source LLC
Chambersburg PA
CBHW070902120626
46546CB00001B/101